CALL to CELEBRATE
CONFIRMATION

Harcourt Religion Publishers
www.harcourtreligion.com

The Ad Hoc Committee to Oversee the Use of the Catechism, United States Conference of Catholic Bishops, has found this catechetical text, copyright 2008, to be in conformity, as supplemental catechetical material, with the *Catechism of the Catholic Church.*

Nihil Obstat
Fr. Esau Garcia
Censor Librorum

Imprimatur
✠ Most Rev. Thomas Wenski
Bishop of Orlando
February 1, 2007

The imprimatur is an official declaration that a book or pamphlet is free of doctrinal or moral error. No implication is contained therein that anyone who granted the imprimatur agrees with the contents, opinions, or statements expressed.

Author
Maureen A. Kelly, M.A.

For permission to reprint copyrighted material, grateful acknowledgment is made to the following sources:

Mike Balhoff: Lyrics from "You Have Anointed Me" by Mike Balhoff, Darryl Ducote, and Gary Daigle. Lyrics © 1981 by Damean Music.

Cornell University Press: From "Antiphon for the Holy Spirit" in *Symphonia: A Critical Edition of the 'Symphonia Armonie Celestium Revelationum' (Symphony of the Harmony of Celestial Revelations), Second Edition,* by Hildegard of Bingen, translated by Barbara Newman. Text copyright © 1988, 1998 by Cornell University.

Division of Christian Education of the National Council of the Churches of Christ in the U.S.A.: Scripture quotations from the *New Revised Standard Version Bible: Catholic Edition.* Text copyright © 1993 and 1989 by the Division of Christian Education of the National Council of the Churches of Christ in the U.S.A.

International Commission on English in the Liturgy: From the English translation of *Rite of Confirmation, Rite of Blessing of Oils, Rite of Consecrating the Chrism.* Translation © 1972 by International Committee on English in the Liturgy, Inc. From the English translation of *Rite of Confirmation (Second Edition).* Translation © 1975 by International Committee on English in the Liturgy, Inc. From the English translation of *Book of Blessings.* Translation © 1988 by International Committee on English in the Liturgy, Inc. From the English translation of *Rite of Baptism for Children.* Translation © 1969 by International Committee on English in the Liturgy, Inc. From the English translation of *Holy Communion and Worship of the Eucharist outside Mass.* Translation © 1974 by International Committee on English in the Liturgy, Inc. From the English translation of the *Rite of Christian Initiation of Adults.* Translation © 1985 by International Committee on English in the Liturgy, Inc. From the English translation of "Litany of the Saints" in *The Roman Missal.* Translation © 1973 by International Committee on English in the Liturgy, Inc.

OCP Publications, 5536 NE Hassalo, Portland, OR 97213: Lyrics from "Go Make a Difference" by Steve Angrisano and Thomas Tomaszek. Lyrics © 1997 by Steve Angrisano and Thomas N. Tomaszek. Lyrics from "Somos el Cuerpo de Cristo/We Are the Body of Christ" by Jaime Cortez. Lyrics © 1994 by Jaime Cortez. Lyrics from "We Believe" by Bernadette Farrell. Lyrics © 1993 by Bernadette Farrell. Lyrics from "Turn to Me" by John B. Foley, S. J. Lyrics © 1975 by John B. Foley, S. J. and OCP Publications. Lyrics from "Come, O Spirit of the Lord" (based on Psalm 104) by Tom Kendzia. Lyrics © 1987 by OCP Publications.

Oxford University Press, on behalf of the British Province of the Society of Jesus, www.oup.com: From "God's Grandeur" by Gerard Manley Hopkins in *The Poems of Gerard Manley Hopkins,* edited by W. H. Gardner and N. H. Mackenzie. Published by Oxford University Press, 1970.

Photography Credits:
Front Matter: iv © Royalty Free/Corbis. **Session 1:** 1 Getty Images/1211; 2 Getty Images/BS15040; 3 Stockdisc; 4 SW Productions Brand X Pictures; 5 WP Wittman Ltd.; 9 WP Wittman Ltd.; 10 (top) Carmelite Order of the Netherlands; 10 (bottom) ©Michael Newman/Photo Edit; 11 (top) ©Michelle D. Bridwell/Photo Edit; 11 (bottom) Gene Plaisted, The Crosiers; 12 SW Productions Brand X Pictures. **Session 2:** 15 Harcourt owned; 16 Gene Plaisted, The Crosiers; 17 John Langford/HRW Photo; 18 SW Productions/Getty Images; 19 Gene Plaisted, The Crosiers; 20 Getty Images/590085; 22 ©Syracuse Newspapers/Alastair Halliday/The Image Works; 24 (top) AP/Wide World Photos; 24 (bottom) Getty Images/2151; 25 (top) Harcourt owned; 25 (bottom) © SuperStock, Inc./SuperStock; 26 © Royalty-Free/Corbis. **Session 3:** 29 PhotoDisc; 31 Gene Plaisted, The Crosiers; 32 WP Wittman Ltd.; 33 A. Paul Herrera/Harcourt owned; 35 © The Trustees of the Chester Beatty Library, Dublin/The Bridgeman Art Library; 37 WP Wittman Ltd.; 38 (top) © Collection of the New-York Historical Society, USA/The Bridgeman Art Library; 38 (bottom) Harcourt owned; 39 (top) © Corbis; 39 (bottom) © Martin Meyer/zefa/Corbis; 40 Getty Images/63066. **Session 4:** 43 Getty Images/BS15003; 44 SW Productions Brand X Pictures; 45 © Royalty-Free/Corbis; 46 SW Productions Brand X Pictures; 47 Gene Plaisted, The Crosiers; 49 Getty Images/AA053443; 50 SW Productions Brand X Pictures; 51 SW Productions Brand X Pictures; 52 (top) By Robert Lentz, ofm, courtesy of www.trinitystores.com; 52 (bottom) © Royalty-Free/Corbis; 53 (top) Royalty-Free/Corbis; 53 (bottom) richerimages.com/Photis/JupiterImages; 54 Getty Images/590061. **Session 5:** 57 Gene Plaisted, The Crosiers; 58 Gene Plaisted, The Crosiers; 59 ©David Young-Wolff/Photo Edit; 60 Harcourt owned; 61 Gene Plaisted, The Crosiers; 62 The Granger Collection, New York; 64 SW Productions Brand X Pictures; 65 © Valeta Orlando; 66 (top) Courtesy of Special Collections, Raynor Memorial Libraries, Marquette University; 66 (bottom) © Corbis; 67 (top) Digital Stock; 67 (bottom) Harcourt owned; 68 SW Productions Brand X Pictures. **Session 6:** 71 © Royalty-Free/Corbis; 72 © Royalty-Free/Corbis; 73 eStock Photo/Alamy; 74 Harcourt owned; 75 Gary Russ/HRW; 77 Harcourt Owned; 78 WP Wittman Ltd.; 79 Kunsthistorisches Museum, Vienna, Austria, Giraudon/Bridgeman Art Library; 80 (top) Painting by Kathy Crosse courtesy of ProVision; 80 (bottom) Getty Images/20271; 81 (top) Harcourt owned; 81 (bottom) John Langford/HRW Photo; 82 SW Productions Brand X Pictures. **Session 7:** 85 Harcourt owned; 87 © Michael Pole/CORBIS; 88 © Royalty-Free/Corbis; 89 WP Wittman Ltd.; 90 © SuperStock, Inc./SuperStock; 92 © Pete Leonard/zefa/Corbis; 94 (top) The Art Archive/San Francesco Assisi/Dagli Orti (A); 94 (bottom) © Leonard de Selva/CORBIS; 95 (top) Getty Images/75176; 95 (bottom) Andersen Ross/Brand X Pictures/JupiterImages; 96 Harcourt owned. **Session 8:** 99 © World Films Enterprises/CORBIS; 100 Getty Images/20270; 101 ©Myrleen Ferguson Cate/Photo Edit; 102 John Langford/HRW Photo; 103 © Rob Lewine/CORBIS; 105 Cameraphoto/Art Resource, NY; 106 WP Wittman Ltd.; 108 (top) © POLAK MATTHEW/CORBIS SYGMA; 108 (bottom) Tim Graham/Getty Images; 109 (top) Harcourt owned; 109 (bottom) © Layne Kennedy/CORBIS; 110 Don Couch/HRW Photo. **Back Matter:** 123 © Valeta Orlando; 125 Harcourt Owned; 126 Victoria Smith/HRW; 127 Harcourt owned; 130 Harcourt owned; 132 Harcourt owned; 133 Harcourt owned.

Printed in the United States of America

ISBN 0-15-901662-2

3 4 5 6 7 8 9 10 059 11 10 09 08

Table of Contents

Online Resource Center

Visit **www.harcourtreligion.com** to find Research Links, Q & As, Activities, and Life Connections.

Dear Candidate,

You are preparing to take another step on your **journey of faith**. In Baptism you became a "new creation" in Christ and received the gift and presence of the Holy Spirit to guide you. Your parents and godparents have kept their promises to care for you and bring you up in the practice of the faith. Your catechists, classmates, and other members of the Church have helped you live as a follower of Jesus. You have grown in your understanding of Jesus' message and mission and how it applies to your own life. Every week you participate in the Eucharist and are nourished and strengthened by the Body and Blood of Jesus to respond to your baptismal call to become a **child of the light**. Now you are ready to complete your initiation through the **Sacrament of Confirmation**.

You have already learned much about your faith, participated in the life of the Church, and lived as a disciple of Jesus.

- What do you think will be most helpful for you as you prepare to celebrate the Sacrament of Confirmation?
- What questions do you have about being confirmed?

You will learn more about:

- the Sacraments of Initiation
- the role of the Holy Spirit in your life
- the Gifts of the Holy Spirit
- what it means to be called to holiness and witness
- the signs and symbols of the Roman Catholic Church
- how to pray and reflect

session 1

Journey with the Spirit

I promise you!

This is a phrase we have heard and uttered from childhood.

You have such promise.

We hear these words when someone sees in us or in another the beginnings of something good or great. We have potential to be nurtured and cultivated.

Keeping and breaking promises

Our attitude and our actions toward keeping and breaking promises say something about the depth of truth and honesty that we possess. Keeping promises when self-sacrifice is involved is difficult but courageous. Breaking promises when self-centeredness is involved is easy and cowardly.

What is your experience with making promises?

How do you follow up on promises you make?

Gathering Rite

Procession with the Word

Sing together.

Wade in the water,
wade in the water, children now.
Wade in the water,
God's gonna trouble the water.

Leader: Let us pray.

All: *Pray the Sign of the Cross together.*

Leader: Lord, our God, we gather together as a people on a journey. Open us to understand your longing and love for us; help us both know and depend on your promises to be with us on this journey. We give you praise and thanks for the gift of our Baptism and the presence of the Holy Spirit in us.

All: Amen.

Celebration of the Word

Leader: A reading from the Book of the prophet Jeremiah.
Read Jeremiah 1:4–10.
The word of the Lord.

All: Thanks be to God.

Reflect silently.

What do Jeremiah's words about his age mean to you and what do they say to you about your own faith journey?

RITUAL FOCUS

Renewal of Baptismal Promises

Come forward as directed.

Leader: Heavenly Father, at Baptism, we were joined to you, your Son Jesus Christ, and your Holy Spirit. We were welcomed into the family of the Church. Hear our prayer as we remember our Baptism. We ask this through your Son, Jesus, who lives and reigns forever.

All: Amen.

Renunciation of Sin

Leader: Do you reject sin, so as to live in the freedom of God's children?

All: I do.

Leader: Do you reject the glamour of evil and refuse to be mastered by sin?

All: I do.

Leader: Do you reject Satan, father of sin and prince of darkness?

All: I do.

Profession of Faith

Leader: Do you believe in God the Father almighty, creator of heaven and earth?

All: I do.

Leader: Do you believe in Jesus Christ, his only Son, our Lord?

All: I do.

Leader: Do you believe in the Holy Spirit, the holy catholic Church, the communion of saints, the forgiveness of sins, the resurrection of the body, and life everlasting?

All: I do.

Rite of Christian Initiation, 224–225

Leader sprinkles group with holy water.

Pray the Sign of the Cross as you are sprinkled with holy water.

General Intercessions

Leader: Let us pray.

Reader 1: That with every passing day we come to know Christ more fully, we pray to the Lord.

All: Hear us, O Lord.

Reader 2: That we will be open and generous in our response to this time of preparation, we pray to the Lord.

All: Hear us, O Lord.

Reader 3: That we will find in the Church and among ourselves, signs of unity and unconditional love, we pray to the Lord.

All: Hear us, O Lord.

Reader 4: That we will become more responsive to the needs of others, we pray to the Lord.

All: Hear us, O Lord.

Leader: Let us pray as Jesus has taught us:

Pray the Lord's Prayer together.

Going Forth

Leader: God, our Loving Father, we stand before you in faith. Send your Holy Spirit that we may act as witnesses of that faith to those around us. We ask this through Christ our Lord.

All: Amen.

Sing again the opening song.

Baptismal Promises

Reflect on the Celebration

Your Confirmation Reflections

Use these phrases as a starting point for personal reflection.

*The most significant thing about renewing my baptismal promises today was . . .

*I affirm my belief in God and the faith of the Church in public by . . .

*Participation in the celebration taught me . . .

Faith Sharing

With a partner or in a small group, reread the words of the Renunciation of Sin and Profession of Faith and discuss the following questions:

- How is evil glamorous or how can glamour be evil?
- Why are openness and generosity important virtues for Confirmation preparation?
- What actions can you take as a group to grow as a community of faith?

SYMBOL OF THE HOLY SPIRIT

Water Water is a universal symbol of life and death. Humans grow from fetuses to infants in their mothers' wombs. Birthing thrusts us out of the water of that womb into a new and different life in this world. Water calls forth new life in nature, and it has a cleansing purpose in a variety of situations. Water can also destroy, as it does in floods, tsunamis, and tidal waves. The Old Testament has many water stories:

- Creation, Genesis 1: 20
- Noah and the Flood, Genesis 7–8
- The First Plague, Exodus 7:14–25
- Crossing of the Red Sea, Genesis 14
- Sprinkling of Water, Ezekiel 36:25

Read the Scripture passages cited above.

What do they tell you about the religious symbolism of water?

Water is a symbol of the Holy Spirit because it reminds us that the Holy Spirit acts in Baptism. During Baptism, the priest or deacon prays that the Holy Spirit will confer the grace of Jesus, God's Son, on the water. Through the power of the Holy Spirit, the water becomes the source of new divine life in Christ for us, and in the waters of Baptism, the Holy Spirit gives us divine life.

What did the experience of being sprinkled with water during the celebration mean for you?

Baptismal Promises

When we are baptized as infants or very young children, we are not able to make our baptismal promises as we can when we are older. So, our parents and godparents pledge

- to accept the responsibility of training us in the practice of the faith
- to bring us up to keep God's commandments, by loving him and our neighbor
- to keep us safe from sin so God's life in us will grow stronger

Our parents and godparents renew their baptismal promises as a sign that they are ready to fulfill their pledge. Since your Baptism, you have probably renewed your own baptismal promises at Easter or during a Eucharist that included a Baptism.

REFLECT

Think about promises you have made to others. On a scale of 1 to 10, rank your ability to make and keep promises. How much do you think about your promises before or after you make them? How do you feel when you break a promise?

God's Promise

A promise is a pledge or assurance. We expect people to keep their promises, and we are disappointed when they do not. In Baptism we make promises to God through the Church. But it is important to remember that God first made us a promise. His promise was first made in a *covenant* with the human race. A covenant is a solemn and mutual agreement between people or between God and a person or community. In a covenant agreement, both God and the persons involved make commitments to one another. In God's covenant with us,

- God promises his presence and faithfulness.
- He invites us to be his children.
- He gives us the gift of *grace*, which is a share in his own life. Grace helps us respond to the baptismal call to become God's adopted children.
- We promise that we will turn from sin and be faithful to God the Father, God the Son, and God the Holy Spirit.

Every time we renew our baptismal promises, we celebrate and remember God's promise. We also renew our own promises to be faithful to him.

DISCUSS

What unique behaviors would you expect of baptized Christians living in today's culture?

God's Covenant

SCRIPTURE BACKGROUND

Covenant The concept of *berith*, the Hebrew word for *covenant*, was in widespread use in the ancient Near East long before Israel used it to describe its unique relationship with Yahweh. These covenants between partners specified both the rights and the responsibilities of each partner. The covenants were often accompanied by litanies of blessings and curses: blessings for those who kept the covenant and curses for those who broke it.

FAITH FOCUS

What is God's covenant?

In the beginning, God created humans in his own image and likeness. This doesn't mean we look like God or he looks like us. It means that God's Spirit dwells within us. Because of this, we are capable of friendship or communion with God. To be created in God's image and likeness is both a gift and a responsibility.

We know that in the beginning, humans were in harmony with God, with one another, and with all of creation. But then something happened. Our first parents, Adam and Eve, disobeyed God. We refer to their sinful action as *original sin*. It disrupted the relationship that humans had with God and disrupted nature's harmony and balance. Because of original sin, human nature is weakened and we are more inclined to sin, which hurts our relationships with God, one another, and creation. The potential to love remains, however, because human life is sacred, each of us created in God's image and likeness.

We read in the Old Testament that God continued to call people into relationship with himself, even after they sinned and turned away from him. God established a covenant with Noah that "never again shall all flesh be cut off by the waters of a flood" (*Genesis 9:11*). God promised to a childless Abram that "I will make of you a great nation, and I will bless you" (*Genesis 12:2*). And God promised Abram that he would give his descendants the land of Canaan. (See *Genesis 12:7*.) Abram's descendants are God's Chosen People. God's gift of the Promised Land followed from his covenant with Abram.

As the Chosen People lived out their lives with God, they wandered in and out of friendship with him. However, he remained faithful to his promise. The people were exiled to Egypt, and God called Moses to lead them to freedom and the Promised Land. During their long journey to the Promised Land, God established another covenant with them on Mount Sinai when he gave Moses the Ten Commandments. The covenant of the Ten Commandments at Mount Sinai demanded a response on the part of the people: "I hereby make a covenant. . . . I will perform marvels, such as have not been performed in all the earth. . . . Observe what I command you today" (*Exodus 34:10–11*).

Promised Land

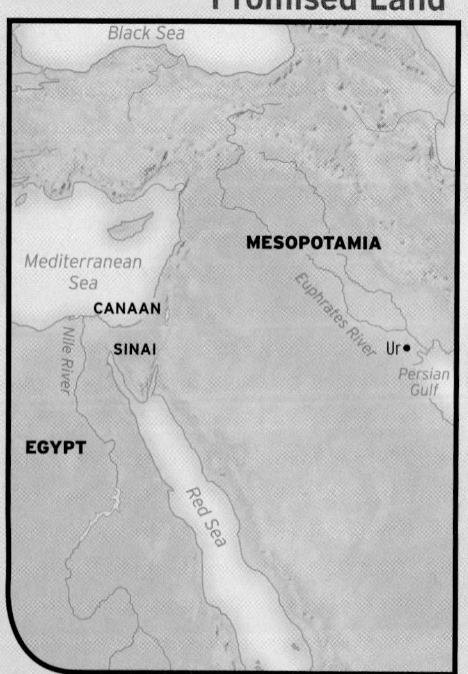

The New Covenant

The story of God and his people is a story of promises made and promises broken on the part of God's people. It is also a story of God's continued faithfulness. The greatest covenant of God was yet to come. He was coming to dwell among humans through his own Son, Jesus. We read in the Old Testament that the prophets prepared the way.

DISCUSS

With a partner or a small group, list the characteristics of God as a covenant maker and keeper.

Written in Hearts

The days are surely coming, says the LORD, when I will make a new covenant with the house of Israel and the house of Judah. It will not be like the covenant that I made with their ancestors when I took them by the hand to bring them out of the land of Egypt—a covenant that they broke, though I was their husband, says the LORD. But this is the covenant that I will make with the house of Israel after those days, says the LORD: I will put my law within them, and I will write it on their hearts; and I will be their God, and they shall be my people. No longer shall they teach one another, or say to each other, "Know the LORD," for they shall all know me, from the least of them to the greatest, says the LORD; for I will forgive their iniquity and remember their sin no more.

—Jeremiah 31:31–34

How will the new covenant be different from the covenant made with Abram? How will it be the same?

What steps have you taken to develop a relationship with God?

Share the Word

But I say to you From the beginning, God's unconditional love is the basis of the covenant. The Jewish people saw the keeping of the Law as part of their covenant responsibility. In the Gospels, Jesus challenges his listeners to imitate God the Father's unconditional love in their response to the covenant. Read Matthew 5:17–48 and discuss how this passage calls us to unconditional responses.

A Covenant People

CATHOLIC SOURCES

Encyclicals are letters written by the Pope and circulated (the Greek root word for *encyclical* means "circular") to all the bishops of Christendom or to all the bishops in a particular country. They are intended to guide the bishops in their relationships with the faithful. Encyclicals are first released in Latin. The titles used to refer to them come from the first few words of the document.

Several encyclicals about the Church are

- ***Ecclesiam Suam***—a letter on the ways the Church must carry out her mission in the contemporary world (Pope Paul VI, August 6, 1964)
- ***Ut Unum Sint***—a letter on the Church and ecumenism (Pope John Paul II, May 25, 1995)
- ***Ecclesia De Eucharistia***—a letter on the Eucharist and its relationship to the Church (Pope John Paul II, April 17, 2003)

FAITH FOCUS

How are we initiated into the Church?

It is challenging for people to be faithful to the covenant. God does not expect us to do this by ourselves. He gives us a community of believers to help us. That community is the Church, the People of God.

Church as Sacrament

The word *church* means *convocation* or an assembly of people who are called together by God's word and the sacraments. The Church is visible, especially as she gathers together for worship and her members live out the promises of their Baptism every day through:

- worshiping God
- praying
- taking care of the needs of those who are sick or poor
- living good lives based on the teachings of Jesus

Through Christian witness, people come to know God's presence in the world. In these ways, the visible Church shows the invisible presence of God. Because of this, we say the Church is a sacrament.

As members of the Church, we come to know God's promises, and we are strengthened by the power and presence of the Holy Spirit who accompanies us on our life journey. He forms us as disciples and helps us live out our baptismal promises.

Initiation

Belonging to the Church is somewhat like belonging to other groups. You gradually come to know others and become known. You learn about the symbols and rituals of the group. You learn what behavior is acceptable and what is not. You come to know what the group believes and values, and you determine whether these beliefs and values match your own. It takes time being with the group before you really belong. Depending on the group, there may be special ceremonies that celebrate your belonging or place in the group. These celebrations are rites of initiation. Initiation means becoming a member. But it's important to realize that being a member of the Church is much more than belonging to any other group.

The Sacraments of Initiation

We meet the living God in all of the *sacraments*. But it is through the *Sacraments of Initiation*—Baptism, Confirmation, and Eucharist—that we are introduced to God's covenant of love and enabled to live it out in a deep relationship with God the Father, God the Son, and God the Holy Spirit, who comes to dwell within us. Through these sacraments, we become full members of the Church.

Baptism takes away original sin and any personal sins committed; it makes us adopted children of God, members of the Body of Christ, and Temples of the Holy Spirit. *Confirmation* completes the graces received in Baptism. Through it we receive the special strength of the *Holy Spirit* who helps us become stronger children of God and members of the Church. Baptism and Confirmation imprint an indelible mark on the Christian. They may be received only once in a person's lifetime. The *Eucharist*, which is the "source and summit" of the Christian's life, completes Christian initiation. The Eucharist is celebrated daily, and participation is so important that we are required to attend Mass on Sundays. With it we grow closer to Jesus and are strengthened to go out and bring his message to others.

Baptism and Confirmation are not always celebrated separately. When adults come into the Church through the Rite of Christian Initiation of Adults, they receive the three Sacraments of Initiation at the same time. This was the custom of the early Church, and even today Eastern Catholic Churches receive all three Sacraments of Initiation in the same celebration. Today the Confirmation of previously baptized people is celebrated at different ages and times of the year. When Confirmation is separated from Baptism, the candidates always renew their baptismal promises. Confirmation, celebrated during the celebration of Mass, reflects the unity of the Sacraments of Initiation.

REFLECT

The person you choose as your Confirmation sponsor must be a confirmed, practicing Catholic. The role of the sponsor is to present you for anointing during the celebration of Confirmation and help you fulfill your baptismal promises during the rest of your life. What faith qualities do you think your sponsor must have?

SIGNS OF FAITH

Baptismal and Confirmation Names Being called by name and having one's name changed to indicate a change were important biblical experiences.

God names the animals.	Genesis 2:20
The people praise God's name.	Psalm 68:5
Simon becomes Peter.	John 1:42

In what ways do these Scripture passages emphasize the importance of names?

In some parishes, those to be confirmed choose a Confirmation name based on a saint who serves as their patron or advocate. Although this is not a part of the Rite, it is a popular devotion in some communities. You can read more about Choosing a Name on page 125.

 **How would you describe the relationship of your own name to your Catholic identity?**

Witnesses of Faith

Journeys Past

Blessed Titus Brandsma
(1881–1942)

1881 Ano Sjoera Brandsma is born at Bolsward, Friesland, Holland.

1899 He joins the Carmelite Friars at Boxmeer and takes the name Titus.

1901 Titus translates the works of Saint Teresa of Avila from Spanish to Dutch.

1905 Titus is ordained a Carmelite priest at age twenty-four.

1909 He receives a doctorate in philosophy from the Pontifical Gregorian University in Rome and teaches at the Carmelite seminary at Oss, Netherlands.

1919 He becomes the editor of the local daily newspaper, where he is often seen working with a cigar in his mouth.

1923 He is named professor of philosophy and of the history of mysticism in the Catholic University of Nijmegen, where he also serves as rector and is well liked by the students.

1932 Titus becoms president of the university.

1935 He is appointed ecclesiastical adviser to Catholic journalists. He writes against anti-Jewish marriage laws, which brings him to the attention of the Nazis. He later writes that no Catholic publication could publish Nazi propaganda and still call itself Catholic. Titus conducts a speaking tour throughout the United States. He visits Niagara Falls and is continually followed by the Gestapo.

1942 In January, Titus is arrested by the Nazis. For several weeks, he is shuttled from jail to jail, where he is abused and punished for ministering to other prisoners. In July, he dies by lethal injection at the Dachau concentration camp.

1985 Titus is beatified by Pope John Paul II.

"Not my will but yours be done!"

Titus shouted these words during his torture by the Nazis.

Your Journey

Faith in Action

Catholic Social Teachings

The waters of Baptism, the fire of Confirmation, and God's new covenant of the Eucharist call all Christians to promote justice. Like Jeremiah, we can't use our age as an excuse for not speaking up for those victims of injustice that we encounter on our journey through life. Like Blessed Titus Brandsma, with our eyes and hearts open to see injustice and to care for its victims, we can put our concerns into writing. No high school student is too young to write letters to the editor of the local newspaper expressing his or her concerns about health care, education, or housing for those denied these basic rights.

Visit **www.harcourtreligion.com** to discover more about Catholic social teachings.

Journeys Today

Living Witness

I was lucky to attend a high school that offered a religion course for seniors called "Prayer & Meditation." It was a workshop based on the Spiritual Exercises of Saint Ignatius of Loyola, the founder of the Jesuits. Up until then, my idea of faith had been rather passive—handed down to me from my parents, something to be cherished and admired like an antique. After that class, my faith became something I *practiced*—faith more as a verb than as a noun.

In college, I felt challenged by the stories about Jesus going out of his way to be with people who were poor, vulnerable, or outcasts. So, I got involved in service in the inner city. I came to realize that my Catholic faith makes much more sense from the perspective of those who live on the margins. They have given me new eyes to see the world, and a new heart—broken by the reality of poverty and injustice in our society, but put together anew by generosity, hope, and solidarity.

I wanted a career that would give me the opportunity to practice a faith that seeks justice. After graduate studies in ethics, I found an extraordinary job as the director of a social ministries group. I am responsible for cultivating solidarity and social action among Jesuits and their lay partners who work in education, parishes, and direct social services.

Mark P.

Faith

Faith is a way of seeing things. It gives us a perspective for viewing the world that is different from the perspective of those who do not have the gift of faith. Though faith is a gift of God, it is also a virtue. It grows as we practice it. Through practice, believing in God and following the beliefs of the Church become habits.

Faith Walk

Respond in Faith

Your Confirmation Reflections

*Write about what you want to do to make your preparation time for the Sacrament of Confirmation valuable for you.

*Describe how you see your relationship with your sponsor during this time. Think of it as writing a job description for your sponsor. For help on the role of the sponsor, read Choosing a Sponsor on page 101.

Faith Sharing

In small groups, discuss the part of this session that

- most interested you
- most challenged you

Spend some time in group silence thinking about what this session is calling you to change or strengthen in your relationship with God, yourself, or others. At the appropriate time, share this with the group.

Closing Prayer

God of all faithfulness,
you have made us in your image and likeness;
You have called us by name
and have continued to love us no matter what.
Send your Holy Spirit upon us that we may be faithful
to our baptismal promises and live as your children.
We ask this in the name of Jesus Christ, who is Lord.
Amen.

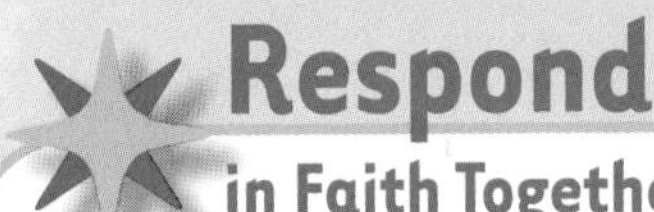

Respond in Faith Together

FAITH FOCUS

Discuss the following beliefs together. Focus on how these beliefs have or could have an effect on your lives today. Refer to the lesson if necessary.

- We are made in the image and likeness of God.
- Original sin brought sin into the world and placed humankind in disordered relationships with God, one another, and creation.
- As a sign and source of God's presence in the world, the Church is a sacrament.

RITUAL FOCUS

During the celebration, the candidates renewed their baptismal promises. At the end of your time together, turn to pages 2–3 and renew your baptismal promises together.

ACT TOGETHER

Together discuss the expectations you each have about the role and responsibility of a sponsor. Review Choosing a Sponsor on page 126. Make a plan on how, when, and what you will do to meet and support your mutual goals.

Your Plan Write about your plan:

BEING CATHOLIC

Together: Read and discuss these quotes from famous Catholics. Focus on how they apply to your life.

"How can we live in harmony? First we need to know we are all madly in love with the same God."

— **Saint Thomas Aquinas**

"The feeling remains that God is on the journey, too."

— **Saint Teresa of Ávila**

"God is not solitude, but perfect communion. For this reason the human person, the image of God, realizes himself or herself in love, which is a sincere gift of self."

— **Pope Benedict XVI**

Faith Walk

Faith Talk about the story in **Journeys Today.**

- Share the practices and events in your lives that have helped your faith grow.
- Discuss how your faith gives you a different moral, political, or ethical perspective from that of someone who does not have faith.

Together: Make a list of three or four people with whom you both are acquainted and discuss how these people reflect the image of God in their daily lives.

Believe with the Spirit

Use of the phrase **"I have great faith in . . ."** implies trust and confidence. Something about the person, the experience, or the object leaves the speaker with no doubt that he, she, or it will come through for them.

When I believe, **I set my heart** on something or someone.

Have faith. This phrase is often used to encourage people to stand firm in the knowledge or hope that a circumstance or a situation will turn out for the good.

- **Which of the three expressions above best describes or comes closest to how you experience your faith in the Risen Christ?**
- **Recall an experience when your faith in the Risen Christ helped you to stand firm.**

Gathering Rite

Procession with the Word

Sing together.

We believe, we believe, we believe.

"We Believe," © 1993, 1994, Bernadette Farrell. Published by OCP Publications

Leader: Let us pray.

All: *Pray the Sign of the Cross together.*

Leader: Lord, our God, we gather together as a people who believe in you and your promises. Open our hearts to know you more and believe in you more fully. Guide us to seek and find you as you continue to make yourself known to us through the Holy Spirit. We give you praise and thanks for the gift of our faith and the presence of the Holy Spirit in us.

All: Amen.

Celebration of the Word

Leader: A reading from the holy Gospel according to Matthew.

All: Glory to you, Lord.

Leader: *Read Matthew 17:14–21.*
The Gospel of the Lord.

All: Praise to you, Lord Jesus Christ.

Reflect silently.

What does the Gospel tell us about the power of faith? What image of nature describes your faith today?

RITUAL FOCUS

Receiving a Candle

Come forward as directed.

Leader: Heavenly Father, at Baptism, we entered into the faith of the Church. We received the Light of Christ. Hear our prayer as we recall our Baptism and seek to deepen our faith. We ask this through your Son, Jesus, who lives and reigns with you and the Holy Spirit forever.

All: Amen.

Leader: [Name], receive the Light of Christ, walk always as a child of the light and keep the flame of faith burning and alive in your heart.

Respond: **I will.**

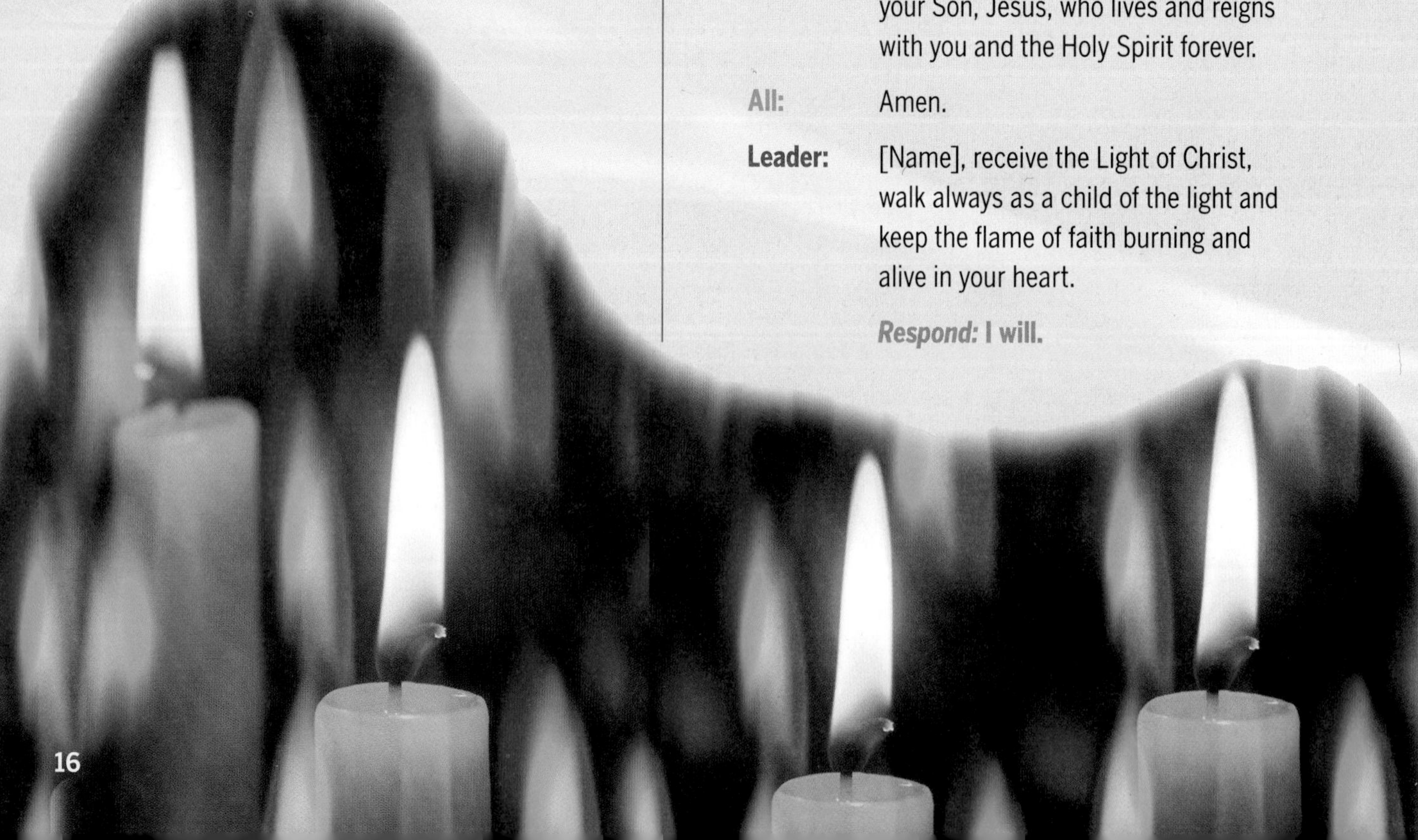

General Intercessions

Leader: Let us pray.

Reader 1: That we will come to a deeper appreciation of the faith we received at Baptism, we pray to the Lord.

All: Hear us, O Lord.

Reader 2: That God will bless us with open eyes and hearts that will come to believe in him more fully and love him more faithfully, we pray to the Lord.

All: Hear us, O Lord.

Reader 3: That we will find, in this community of faith, support and strength to live as children of the light, we pray to the Lord.

All: Hear us, O Lord.

Reader 4: That in faith we will become more responsive to the needs of others, we pray to the Lord.

All: Hear us, O Lord.

Leader: Let us pray as Jesus has taught us:

Pray the Lord's Prayer together.

Going Forth

Leader: God, our Loving Father, we stand before you in faith. Send your Holy Spirit that we may act as witnesses of that faith to those around us. We ask this through Christ our Lord.

All: Amen.

Sing again the opening song.

Light of Christ

Reflect
on the Celebration

Your Confirmation Reflections

Use the following phrases as prompts for reflection:

*During the celebration, I was thinking about . . .

*The call to "walk always as a child of the light" . . .

*The image of faith as a flame . . .

Faith Sharing

With a partner or in a small group, review the four General Intercessions from the celebration. Discuss your experiences and thoughts about appreciating one's Baptism and about the need for a community of faith.

SIGNS OF FAITH

Paschal Candle Light is a primary symbol for Catholics. It is used throughout the Scriptures to describe God's presence and to show that believers have the responsibility to be light for the world.

- The Lord preceded the Israelites into the desert at night as a column of fire. (See *Exodus 13:21.*)
- We walk in the light of the Lord. (See *Isaiah 2:5.*)
- Believers must let their light shine. (See *Matthew 5:14.*)
- We are all children of the light. (See *1 Thessalonians 5:5.*)
- God is the source of all light. (See *Revelations 22:5.*)

Another name for the Paschal Candle is the Easter candle. It is a tall, white candle. During the Easter Vigil, the priest cuts a cross in the candle and traces the Greek letters Alpha above the cross and Omega below, which symbolizes that Jesus is the beginning and the end. Then he carves the numerals of the calendar year into the candle and lights the candle from the Easter fire. While the church is still in darkness, the Paschal Candle is carried in procession into the church as a symbol of the Risen Christ. The candles of the assembly are lit from the Paschal Candle. The Paschal Candle is lit at all the Masses of the Easter season, from Easter through Pentecost, and at Baptisms and funerals throughout the year.

Read the Scripture passages cited above. How would you relate them to your daily living?

The lighting of the Paschal Candle at the Easter Vigil tells a story of faith. List what you think are the important parts of the story.

Enlightened by Christ

During the Baptism of a child, the priest or deacon refers to the Easter candle, which represents the presence of the Risen Christ in the world, and says, "Receive the Light of Christ." Then one of the parents or godparents lights the child's baptismal candle from the Easter candle. The presider tells the parents and godparents to keep the light "burning brightly." He prays that the "flame of faith" will be kept alive in the child's heart. The more the child comes to know the Risen Christ and grows in relationship with him, the more faith grows and the more he or she sees things through the life and teachings of Jesus.

REFLECT

When difficult or senseless things happen, how does your faith help you see things differently from people who do not have faith?

Faith and Light

Light is one of the many images and words the Church uses to describe the mystery of faith. *Faith* is our free response to God, who first shares his great gift of love, and to all that he tells us about himself in revelation. *Revelation* involves God's communication of himself in the Old and New Testaments, and especially through his own Son, Jesus Christ.

We begin to see and understand life better through the light of faith. We can see what we are called to be and do as disciples. Faith is a way of seeing—enlightened by the Risen Christ and guided by the Holy Spirit, we grow to see the world as God does. The Holy Spirit helps us see and hear with the eyes and ears of faith. Through faith, we can discover new possibilities for ourselves and new strengths and talents. We see the world in a different way from those who do not believe.

Seeing and Believing

SCRIPTURE BACKGROUND

The Gospel of John The style of the Gospel of John is very different from the styles of the Gospels of Matthew, Mark, and Luke. This Gospel does not have parables or the Sermon on the Mount. In the Gospel of John, Jesus addresses these audiences: the disciples, the crowds, and his opponents. When reading this Gospel, pay attention to whom Jesus is speaking and notice how differently he approaches each group. Seven miracles are found in this Gospel, and five of the seven are described only in the Gospel of John. All the miracles are intended to call forth faith on the part of those who see them. Sometimes the miracles are followed by a debate with some of the Pharisees.

FAITH FOCUS

What does faith do?

The Gospel of John uses many symbols and images to describe the Good News and the kingdom. Light and darkness are two of these symbols. In the beginning of the Gospel, we hear that Jesus was a light that came into darkness. Later we read that when Jesus instructed Nicodemus about faith, Jesus talked about light and darkness again and referred to himself as the light of the world. In the story of the Man Born Blind, Jesus used light, darkness, and seeing to teach about the mystery of faith. The Jewish people would not believe the man's testimony about Jesus. They drove him out of the town. Jesus found him and said:

"Do you believe in the Son of Man?" He answered, "And who is he, sir? Tell me, so that I may believe in him." Jesus said to him, "You have seen him, and the one speaking with you is he." He said, "Lord, I believe." And he worshiped him. Jesus said, "I came into this world for judgment so that those who do not see may see, and those who do see may become blind."

—John 9:35–39

Maybe it was easier for the man born blind to believe in Jesus because he had experienced the miracle of having his sight restored. But the Pharisees had seen the *miracle*, and they still did not believe. Faith is a gift of God, but it has two sides. God continues to make known his presence and to call humans to a faithful relationship with him. We must choose to recognize and respond to his presence.

When have you recognized and responded to God's call to faith?

Faith and Fear

The Pharisees were not the only people who had a difficult time believing in Jesus; sometimes the Apostles questioned and doubted.

REFLECT

What events and/or occurrences in your life have helped you believe in Jesus? What things might have made it more difficult to believe?

Jesus Stills the Storm

And when he got into the boat, his disciples followed him. A windstorm arose on the sea, so great that the boat was being swamped by the waves; but he was asleep. And they went and woke him up, saying, "Lord, save us! We are perishing!"

And he said to them, "Why are you afraid, you of little faith?" Then he got up and rebuked the winds and the sea; and there was a dead calm.

They were amazed, saying, "What sort of man is this, that even the winds and the sea obey him?"

—Matthew 8:23–27

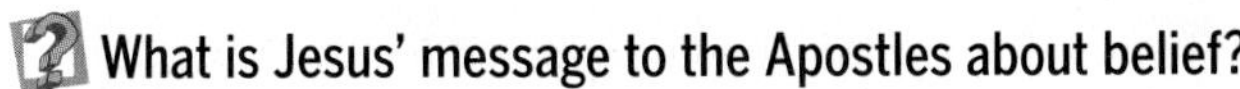

What is Jesus' message to the Apostles about belief?

How can this reading help your faith?

Share the Word

With a partner or in a small group, select two of the Scripture passages below. Read and discuss what they tell you about faith. Then write a paragraph to complete the open-ended sentence that follows.

Matthew 14:28–33	Mark 4:35–42	John 20:24–29
Matthew 15:21–28	Luke 18:35–43	Acts 3:1–10
Matthew 26:69–75	John 14:1–26	Hebrews 11:1–2

These Scriptures helped me see that faith and believing . . .

Personal Faith

DISCUSS

What role does belonging and participating in a Church have in a person's faith journey? What about in *your* faith journey?

FAITH FOCUS

What is the role of the community in faith development?

Faith is a lifelong relationship with God. Each of us has a very personal and unique relationship with him. As your faith continues to deepen, you will see things from a different point of view. You will grow in your trust of God and feel more connected to him and his plan for you and the world. This is what the Sacraments of Initiation celebrate—your new connections and deepening bonds with God and the Church.

Communal Faith

While faith and the celebration of the Sacraments of Initiation are personal acts, they are much more than that. They are actions of the Church. Just as we cannot live alone, we cannot believe alone. We receive our faith from God through other people like our parents and family members, and we hand it on to others. We are all links in the chain of faith. Faith has an important *communal* aspect—we are carried by the faith of others, and we support others in faith through our beliefs, prayers, and actions. It is through the community of the Church that our faith is fed and supported.

The Church

- teaches us the language of faith through prayer and doctrines (official teachings)
- preserves the memory of Jesus' words and actions in the Scriptures and sacraments
- proclaims and maintains the mysteries of faith in the creeds

Guided by the Church and inspired by the Holy Spirit, we grow in both our personal and communal faith through actions such as these:

- talking to God
- reading and thinking about the Scriptures
- participating in the communal worship of church, especially in the sacraments
- going out in service to those in need
- learning more in parish programs

completion of Baptism

The Holy Spirit began the journey of faith with you at Baptism. In Confirmation you will again be blessed with the special Gifts of the Holy Spirit. Confirmation is necessary for the completion of the grace of Baptism. During his homily, the bishop or priest who will confirm you will remind you of your Baptism. He will talk about the importance of your responding to faith in your life.

In these or similar words, he will say the following:

> *You have already been baptized into Christ and now you will receive the power of his Spirit and the Sign of the Cross on your forehead. You must be witnesses before all the world to his suffering, death, and Resurrection; your way of life should at all times reflect the goodness of Christ . . .*
>
> *Be active members of the Church, alive in Jesus Christ. Under the guidance of the Holy Spirit, give your lives completely in the service of all, as did Christ who came not to be served but to serve.*
>
> *So now before you receive the Spirit, I ask you to renew the profession of faith you made in Baptism or your parents or godparents made in union with the whole Church.*
>
> **Rite of Confirmation, 23**

The Sacrament of Confirmation joins you more closely to the Church and gives you a special strength of the Holy Spirit, which will help you share and explain your faith with others in word and action.

CATHOLIC SOURCES

Creeds All Christian creeds refer to the three Persons of the Trinity and are developed from baptismal rituals. These three creeds, or professions of faith, have been used by the Church:

- The Athanasian Creed, which stresses belief in the Incarnation and the Trinity
- The Apostles' Creed, which is the earliest and simplest expression of Christian belief
- The Nicene Creed, which is a combination of the creeds drawn up at the Councils of Nicaea and Constantinople. It summarizes salvation history, and it is the creed ordinarily professed at Sunday liturgies.

SYMBOL OF THE HOLY SPIRIT

Cloud and Light In the Old Testament, the images of cloud and light often appear together when the Lord is revealing himself. With Moses on Mount Sinai (see *Exodus 24:15–18*), the meeting tent (see *Exodus 33:9–10*), and the wandering in the desert (see *Exodus 40:36–38*), the cloud that reveals Yahweh is both radiant and murky. In the New Testament, the Holy Spirit "overshadows" the Virgin Mary at the Annunciation (see *Luke 1:35*); at the Transfiguration (see *Luke 9:34–35*) the cloud overshadows Jesus, Moses, and Elijah; Peter, James, and John hear a voice from the cloud that says: "This is my Son, my Chosen; listen to him!"(*Luke 9:35*).

Cloud and light are almost opposites. Why are they good images for the Holy Spirit?

Witnesses of Faith

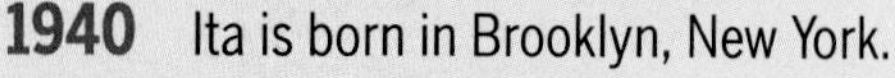

Journeys Past

1940 Ita is born in Brooklyn, New York.

1960 She graduates from Marymount College.

1961 She enters the Maryknoll Sisters.

1964 Ita leaves Maryknoll Missionary Order due to health problems and works awhile as an editor.

1971 She reapplies to Maryknoll and is accepted.

1972 Assigned to the missions in Chile, Ita goes with her friend Sister Carla.

1980 In March, Ita and Carla respond to a call from El Salvador's Bishop Oscar Romero—just before his assassination. In June, they begin working at the Emergency Refugee Committee in Chalatenango. In August, while returning a political prisoner to his home, Ita and Carla are caught in a flash flood. Carla drowns after pushing Ita to safety. Maura Clarke becomes Ita's new missionary partner. At a closing liturgy on December 1 in Nicaragua, Ita reads this passage from one of Archbishop Romero's final homilies: "Christ invites us not to fear persecution because, believe me, brothers and sisters, the one who is committed to the poor must run the same fate as the poor, and in El Salvador we know what the fate of the poor signifies: to disappear, be tortured, to be held captive—and to be found dead."

The following day, Ita and Maura return to El Salvador and are picked up by missionaries Dorothy Kazel, an Ursuline sister, and Jean Donovan, a layperson. After the women leave the airport in San Salvador, several members of the National Guard of El Salvador stop their vehicle and take the four women to an isolated spot where the soldiers rape and murder them.

"Am I willing to suffer with the people here, . . . Can I say to my neighbors, 'I have no solutions to this situation; I don't know the answers, but I will walk with you, search with you, be with you'?"

Your Journey

Solidarity of the Human Family

Faith in Action

The Light of Christ in us at age seventeen may not be as bright as Ita Ford's at age thirty-two or when she began her missionary work with the poor in Chile. But "this light of mine, I'm gonna let it shine!" Like Ita Ford, we can choose to believe that God calls us to be in solidarity with others who are hurting. We can contact Maryknoll's Office of Global Concerns about their work overseas and find out how we can be in solidarity with one of their projects. Maybe together, with others around the world, we can work with such faith and courage that we will move the mountain of injustice at least a little in our lifetime.

Visit **www.harcourtreligion.com** to discover more about Catholic social teachings.

Journeys Today

Living Witness

I am a doctor at a family clinic for the poor in a large Midwestern city. As I see it, I got here by making small choices. In fact, I see my whole life as a series of small choices.

In high school I was very influenced by the Sisters of Loretto, especially in the way they integrated justice and civil rights. In those years, I began to see that there were no boundaries that separated me from any other human being.

I wanted to be a medical missionary. So I chose to go to medical school. During my residency in the deep south, I became aware of terrible injustices and divides between people because of race and economic differences. It threw me off balance and I realized I could not be a doctor there. So I left and went to an inner city hospital that dealt with a bigger world and confronted the inequity of education, healthcare, and benefits. That choice provided me with wonderful mentors who taught me how to think, solve problems, and be creative when it came to caring about others.

When I finished my residency, I went to Thailand to work in a refugee camp. I was a missionary at last, but I soon realized that it was not my calling. It did not fit me and when something doesn't fit, I have learned it is not what God is calling me to. I made the choice to return to the States and found a medical setting where there were no boundaries that separated the poor from good medical care.

Ann S.

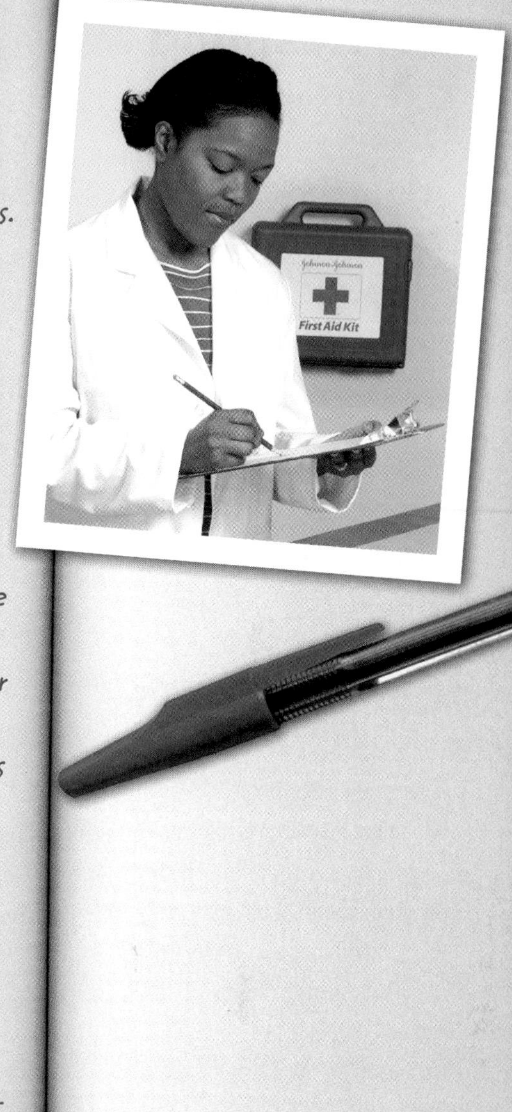

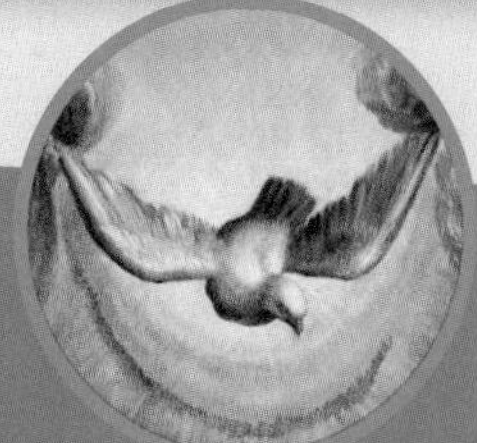

Christian Decision Making

Faith Walk

This is a process of making choices and decisions that are based on faith and the desire to do God's will. It involves being open to the Holy Spirit's guidance and calling on him to lead or enlighten people as to what God wants them to do and be. These are some questions to ask when you are making decisions:

> Is my choice governed by love of God, self, or others?

> Does it use or enhance the gifts and talents God has given me?

> Does it flow from the teachings of the Scriptures and Church doctrine?

Respond in Faith

Your Confirmation Reflections

*Think about the people and events of your life as a faith journey and sketch a map or path naming the people, places, rest stops, destinations, and detours that have been part of your journey.

*Write about one thing you learned in this session that you want to pay attention to for your own faith development.

Faith Sharing

In small groups discuss the part of this session that

- most interested you
- most challenged you

Spend some time in group silence thinking about what this session is calling you to change or strengthen in your relationship with God, yourself, or others. At the appropriate time, share this with the group.

closing prayer

Come, Holy Spirit,
Open my eyes that I may see the events of my life through the eyes of faith.
Open my ears that I may hear the word of God spoken to me.
Open my heart that I may grow more in love with God who has loved me first.
Open my hands and move my feet in faith to serve others.
We ask this in the name of Jesus Christ, who is Lord.
Amen.

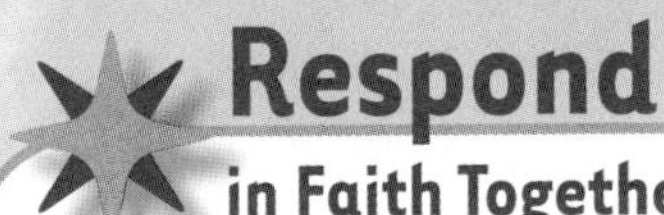

Respond in Faith Together

FAITH FOCUS

Discuss the following beliefs together. Focus on how these beliefs have or could have an effect on your lives today. Refer to the lesson if necessary.

- Faith is based on God's great gift of revelation. Among other things, revelation tells us that God the Father communicated himself and his plan for all creation by sending us his own Son, Jesus.
- Faith has two sides: God's call and our response.
- Being a member of the Church strengthens and supports our faith.

RITUAL FOCUS

During the celebration, the candidates received a candle and were reminded of the call to be children of the light. At the end of your time together, pray together for one another using these or similar words:

May Christ always be our light.
May we walk always as children of the light.
May we see life through the eyes of faith.
May our journey of faith bring light to others.

Amen.

ACT TOGETHER

At the conclusion of the Renewal of Baptismal Promises, the bishop or priest will say these words:

This is our faith. This is the faith of the Church.
We are proud to profess it in Christ Jesus our Lord.

Rite of Confirmation, 23

Together select two persons from the parish community who are witnesses of faith. Set up a conversation with them to discuss how they nurture their faith and how and why they are proud to profess it in their daily lives.

Your Plan Write about your conversation:

BEING CATHOLIC

Together: Discuss these quotes from famous Catholics. Focus on how they apply to your life.

"Faith is to believe what you do not see; the reward of this faith is to see what you believe."

— Saint Augustine

"A strong, lively faith is the foundation of all virtue."

— Catherine McAuley

"Faith has to do with things that are not seen, and hope with things that are not in hand."

— Saint Thomas Aquinas

Faith Walk

Christian decision making Talk about the story in **Journeys Today.**

- Identify areas in your life where making more decisions based on faith would help you.
- Discuss how the Scriptures and Church doctrine affect your daily decision-making.

Together: Reflect on your own faith journey. Recall the people and events that have been significant in the deepening of your faith.

Gifted with the Spirit

Gifts that keep on giving There are different ways to imagine what gifts that keep on giving might be. They might be lifetime subscriptions to a magazine or a service or the gifts of time, talent, and friendship.

The Giving Tree This book by Shel Silverstein is a classic. If you have read it, what do you remember about it? Would you want a tree like this for yourself, or are you taking steps to become one?

Gift of a lifetime This phrase is often used in advertising. It touches a deep longing in humans to be satisfied.

- **What kind of gift is the presence of the Holy Spirit for you?**
- **Recall a time when you felt gifted by God.**

Gathering Rite

Procession with the Word

Sing together.

Come, O Spirit of the Lord,
and renew the face of the earth.
O, come, O Spirit of the Lord,
and renew the face of the earth.

Leader: Let us pray.

All: *Pray the Sign of the Cross together.*

Leader: Lord, may the Helper, the Spirit who comes from you, fill our hearts with light and lead us to all truth as your Son promised, for he lives and reigns with you and the Holy Spirit, one God, forever and ever.

All: Amen.

Votive Mass of the Holy Spirit

Celebration of the Word

Leader: A reading from the First Letter of Paul to the Corinthians.
Read 1 Corinthians 2:6–13.
The word of the Lord.

All: Thanks be to God.

Reflect silently.

What does "God's wisdom" mean for you? How would it help you in your life?

RITUAL FOCUS

Blessing

Come forward as directed.

Leader: Father, as your Spirit guides us and your loving care keeps us safe, be close to us in your mercy and listen to those who call on you. Strengthen and protect by your kindness the faith of all who believe in you. We ask this through our Lord Jesus Christ, your Son, who lives and reigns with you and the Holy Spirit, one God, forever and ever.

All: Amen.

Votive Mass of the Holy Spirit

Leader: *Mark each candidate's forehead with the Sign of the Cross while saying:*

[Name], may you be open to the coming of the fullness of the Holy Spirit.

General Intercessions

Leader: Let us pray.

Reader 1: That we will come to a deeper appreciation of the presence of the Holy Spirit in our lives, we pray to the Lord.

All: Come, Holy Spirit.

Reader 2: That the Holy Spirit will enliven and enlighten us to live as disciples, we pray to the Lord.

All: Come, Holy Spirit.

Reader 3: That the Holy Spirit will pour out his courage on young men and women and raise them up as leaders in the Church and world, we pray to the Lord.

All: Come, Holy Spirit.

Reader 4: That the Holy Spirit will bless us with a wisdom that will allow us to search out and choose just and fair ways of living with all our brothers and sisters, we pray to the Lord.

All: Come, Holy Spirit.

Leader: Let us pray as Jesus has taught us:

Pray the Lord's Prayer together.

Going Forth

Leader: God, our Loving Father, we stand before you in faith. We pray for the fullness of your Holy Spirit that we may live in your love. We ask this through Christ our Lord.

All: Amen.

Sing again the opening song.

Celebrate

The Holy Spirit

Reflect on the Celebration

Your Confirmation Reflections

* Reread the General Intercessions from the celebration.
* Choose the intercession you most identify with and sketch, using words or drawings, a "From—To" page showing how you would be different if the Holy Spirit granted that intercession.

Faith Sharing

With a partner or in a small group, discuss this question:

- When are you aware of the action of the Holy Spirit in your life? In the lives of others?

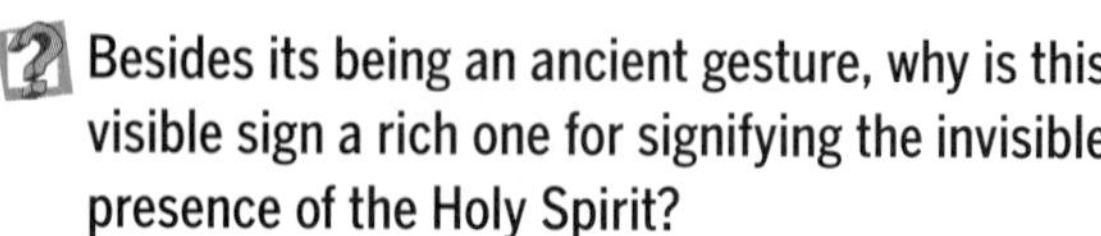

SIGNS OF FAITH

Laying on of Hands The gesture of holding one's hands on or over things or persons to transmit power, duty, or blessing is an ancient gesture. It was used by the Patriarch Jacob to bless his grandsons Ephram and Manas. (See *Genesis 48:14.*) In New Testament accounts, Jesus often laid on hands to heal people. The Apostles laid hands on the newly baptized people so that they would receive the Holy Spirit. (See *Acts 8:17.*)

In Catholic practice today, the gesture is used to invoke the Holy Spirit, especially during the celebration of the sacraments and other forms of blessing or dedication. It is an essential part of the celebration of Holy Orders, when bishops, deacons, and priests are ordained. The gesture is used by the priest at the epiclesis during the Eucharistic Prayer when he invokes the Holy Spirit and prays that the gifts of bread and wine will become the Body and Blood of Christ. It is also used as a sign of Reconciliation in the Rite of Penance.

? Besides its being an ancient gesture, why is this visible sign a rich one for signifying the invisible presence of the Holy Spirit?

? How did the experience of having hands laid on your head and the words "open to the coming of the fullness of the Holy Spirit" affect you?

The Gift of the Holy Spirit

We are not alone as we live out our lives as children of God. In Baptism the Holy Spirit comes to dwell in us. What a wonderful gift! Through the power of the Holy Spirit, we are filled with God's life to heal us from sin and make us holy. We call this life *sanctifying grace*.

The Greek word used in the Scriptures to describe the Holy Spirit is *parakletos*. This Greek word is translated into Latin, using the word *consolator* or *paracletus*. In English it is translated as *paraclete*, advocate or intercessor, teacher, helper, comforter, and consoler.

An *advocate* is someone who supports us and acts on our behalf. Advocates actively encourage us to accomplish our goals. They are on and at our side. In the Holy Spirit, we have a wise companion and an Advocate to journey with us.

REFLECT

There was a time when you could not do many of the things you do today, many of which you probably take for granted. Did you learn these things by yourself, or did you ask for help along the way?

DISCUSS

When and in what ways would you like the Holy Spirit to be an Advocate for you?

Promise of the Holy Spirit

SCRIPTURE BACKGROUND

Pentecost The word *pentecost* comes from the Greek word meaning "fiftieth." In the Old Testament, it is called the Feast of Weeks, and it is one of the three mandatory feasts of the Jewish people. It falls between Passover and the Feast of Tabernacles. It began as an agricultural feast of thanksgiving to God for the harvest and was dated "seven weeks from the time you put the sickle to the standing grain" *(Deuteronomy 16:9)*, thus the reference to fifty. However, by the time of Jesus, the feast lost its agricultural significance and was more associated with the covenant. It was during the celebration of the Feast of Weeks that the Holy Spirit descended on the Apostles. This is probably why so many Jewish people were in Jerusalem at the time. Christians use the term *Pentecost* to refer to the first coming of the Holy Spirit upon the Apostles fifty days after Easter.

FAITH FOCUS

Why did Jesus promise to send the Holy Spirit?

As Jesus was preparing for his death, he encouraged the Apostles with the promise of the Holy Spirit.

Another Advocate

"If you love me, you will keep my commandments. And I will ask the Father, and he will give you another Advocate, to be with you forever. This is the Spirit of truth, whom the world cannot receive, because it neither sees him nor knows him. You know him, because he abides with you, and he will be in you.

"I will not leave you orphaned; I am coming to you. In a little while the world will no longer see me, but you will see me; because I live, you also will live. On that day you will know that I am in my Father, and you in me, and I in you. . . .

"I have said these things to you while I am still with you. But the Advocate, the Holy Spirit, whom the Father will send in my name, will teach you everything, and remind you of all that I have said to you. Peace I leave with you; my peace I give to you. I do not give to you as the world gives. Do not let your hearts be troubled, and do not let them be afraid. You heard me say to you, 'I am going away, and I am coming to you.' If you loved me, you would rejoice that I am going to the Father, because the Father is greater than I. And now I have told you this before it occurs, so that when it does occur, you may believe."

—John 14:15–20, 25–29

Why did the Apostles need encouragement?

In what ways do you want the Holy Spirit to be an Advocate for you?

Gift for the Church

We read in the Old Testament that the prophets stressed that the Spirit of the Lord would rest on the expected Messiah and would guide the Messiah's mission. (See *Isaiah 11:2, 6:1.*) The New Testament proclaims the fulfillment of those prophecies in Jesus. (See *Matthew 1:18, 3:13–17.*) His promise to send the Holy Spirit shows us that the gift of the Spirit was not just for Jesus and his mission, but for the whole Church. It also reminds us that the work of God the Son and God the Holy Spirit are inseparable; when God the Father sends one, he sends the other.

Jesus' promise was fulfilled at Pentecost and from that time on, the Apostles and those who followed them passed on the gift of the Holy Spirit to the newly baptized by the laying on of hands.

Pentecost, by Simon Bening (c. 1530)

Share the Word

Read the following passages that describe titles of the Holy Spirit. Choose one of the titles and, in the space provided, write your own personal prayer to the Holy Spirit using that title. In groups of three or four, explain why you chose the title you did and share your prayer.

TITLES OF THE HOLY SPIRIT

Title	Passage	
Spirit of Truth	John 16:13	
Spirit of Promise	Galatians 3:14	
Spirit of Adoption	Romans 8:15	
Spirit of Christ	1 Peter 1:10–11	
Spirit of the Lord	2 Corinthians 3:17	
Spirit of God	Romans 8:9–14	
Spirit of Glory	1 Peter 4:14	

The Trinity

REFLECT

When you pray, how do you visualize God?

DISCUSS

With a partner or in a small group, name and talk about which Person of the Trinity you pray to most often.

CATHOLIC SOURCES

Joint Commission for the Theological Dialogue between the Roman Catholic Church and the Orthodox Church "The church finds its model, its origin and its purpose in the mystery of God, one in three persons. Further still, the eucharist thus understood in the light of the Trinitarian mystery is the criterion for functioning of the life of the church as a whole. The institutional elements should be nothing but a visible reflection of the reality of the mystery."

FAITH FOCUS

What is the work of the Holy Spirit?

The Holy Spirit is the third Person of the Holy Trinity. *Trinity* is the name the Church gives to the mystery of one God in three Persons—Father, Son, and Holy Spirit. It is really impossible for us to understand this central mystery of our faith with our human minds. God is bigger than anything we can understand or any words we can use to describe him. But we can still know him because he has made himself known to us.

When we look at creation or what Jesus told us about God the Father, we get some hints. When we reflect on Jesus who himself is the visible image of the invisible God, we get some hints. When we read about the Apostles at Pentecost and what happened to them afterward, or when we experience the power and presence of the Holy Spirit in our own lives, we get more hints. When we reflect on the symbols of the Trinity, we get even more hints about the mystery of three Persons in one God and how they always are together, yet they remain unique and distinct in who they are.

The Work of the Holy Spirit

The Holy Spirit is God alive in us and in the world. Through the power and presence of the Holy Spirit, we come to know that God does really love us; we come to know who Jesus is and develop a relationship with him; we become members of his Church, the Body of Christ; and we are given the strength to do things similar to those that Jesus did as we continue his mission here on earth.

Pour Out the Holy Spirit

The Holy Spirit began the journey of faith with you at Baptism. In Confirmation you will be blessed with the special strength of the Holy Spirit. Confirmation is necessary to receive the completion of the grace of Baptism. Before the laying on of hands, the bishop addresses the community and asks for the outpouring of the Holy Spirit.

> *My dear friends:*
> *In baptism God our Father gave the new birth of*
> *eternal life to his chosen sons and daughters.*
> *Let us pray to our Father*
> *that he will pour out the Holy Spirit*
> *to strengthen his sons and daughters with his gifts*
> *and anoint them to be more like Christ the Son of God.*

Rite of Confirmation, 24

SYMBOL OF THE HOLY SPIRIT

Wind Wind is moving fresh air. While wind is an unseen force, we can see its effects. It can be powerful, and it cannot be controlled by humans. But it can also be very gentle. The descent of the Holy Spirit was accompanied by "a sound like the rush of a violent wind" (*Acts 2:2*). Jesus speaks of it to Nicodemus and uses the image of wind to talk about those who are "born of the Spirit" (*John 3:8*). He says that like them, "the wind blows where it chooses" (*John 3:8*).

 **Which quality of wind best describes how you experience the power of the Holy Spirit in your life? Why?**

Witnesses of Faith

Journeys Past

Venerable Pierre Toussaint (1778-1853)

Pierre Toussaint, by Anthony Meucci (c. 1825)

1778 Pierre Toussaint is born in Saint Domingue, now Haiti.

1787 He moves to New York City as a house servant for the Berard family. They arrange for Pierre to learn the trade of hairdressing. When Mr. Berard dies and leaves his wife with no money, Pierre provides her with financial support.

1807 On her deathbead, Mrs. Berard gives Pierre his freedom.

1811–1851 He marries Juliette Noel, who also began her life as a slave in Haiti. Together they continue the charitable work Pierre has begun, helping refugees find jobs and caring for orphans. Pierre founds one of New York City's first orphanages with Elizabeth Ann Seton, and he helps raise funds for the city's first cathedral. He and Juliette open a school to teach black children a trade. When the plague strikes New York, Pierre personally cares for the victims. When his sister, Rosalie, dies leaving an orphaned young daughter, Euphemia, Pierre and Juliette welcome her into their home.

1851 Juliette dies.

1853 Pierre dies.

1996 He is declared Venerable by Pope John Paul II.

In view of his lifelong commitment to helping others, Pierre Toussaint is credited as a founder of Catholic charitable works in the United States.

Your Journey

Faith in Action

Call to Family, Community, and Participation

God has given us his Spirit. That's why we don't think (and act) the same way the people of this world think. The Spirit works in the world by inviting us to participate more fully in our family and community. Like Venerable Pierre Toussaint, we can reach out to those who are sick and dying in our extended family and community. Most assisted-living facility residents love to have young people visit them. Some hospice programs need high school volunteers to videotape the life stories of their patients. These are things you can volunteer to do.

Visit **www.harcourtreligion.com** to discover more about Catholic social teachings.

Journeys Today

Living Witness

I am a wife and the mother of two beautiful young girls. I teach 9th grade Religious Studies at an all-girls' Catholic high school. I see my vocation and life work today as providing a safe, affirming, open, and nurturing environment for girls and young women. There was a long period in my life when I did not have a clue about what I was called to do or be. But fortunately I've had a lot of "aha" moments in my life.

Due to my upbringing, it was hard for me to see myself as capable and valuable. However, as a result of deep loneliness in my childhood, I became much more aware of the presence of God in my life. Lucky for me I was able to ask the questions: "What am I supposed to learn from this?" "What am I here for?"

Through my own experiences as a child and meeting loneliness and isolation in others when I worked as a Jesuit volunteer and with the homeless, I realized how important it was to share my faith questions and experiences with others who are traveling a faith journey. I consider these people my spiritual companions. Talking, listening, and praying with these people helps me discern when and where God is calling me.

Bridgid D.

Spiritual Companioning

Faith Walk

This is a method for helping a person develop a personal relationship with God. With the help of a spiritual companion or as part of a small group, the person who takes this spiritual journey learns to become more aware of God's presence in every facet of daily life. The spiritual companion listens and lends support as the person discovers and learns to respond to God's voice and other signs of his activity in the everyday occurrences of ordinary life. The process might include learning to pray, to recognize God's guidance, and to make decisions through discernment. Through spiritual companioning, we seek to ultimately trust God in all things.

Respond in Faith

Your Confirmation Reflections

*Use your own ideas and insights about this session to create a word collage that expresses what you have learned about the Holy Spirit.

*Write about the areas of your life in which you most need the Holy Spirit.

*Choose one of the Scripture passages from this session, meditate on it on four separate days, and record your insights.

Faith Sharing

In small groups, discuss the part of this session that

- most interested you
- most challenged you

Spend some time in group silence thinking about what this session is calling you to change or strengthen in your relationship with God, yourself, or others. At the appropriate time, share this with the group.

closing prayer

Come, Holy Spirit, live in us.
Come with your grace, your power, and your wisdom.
Be our Advocate and counselor.
Guide us to lead lives worthy of our calling.
Amen.

Respond in Faith Together

FAITH FOCUS

Discuss the following beliefs together. Focus on how these beliefs have or could have an effect on your lives today. Refer to the lesson if necessary.

- Through the power of the Holy Spirit, we are filled with God's life.
- The Holy Spirit is our Advocate.
- Trinity is the name the Church gives to the mystery of one God in three Persons—Father, Son, and Holy Spirit.

RITUAL FOCUS

During the celebration, candidates experienced a laying on or imposition of hands and a prayer of blessing. At the end of your time together, place your right hand on your candidate's head and pray the following prayer:

Father,
As your Spirit guides us and your
loving care keeps us safe, be close to [Name].
Strengthen and protect by your kindness
the faith of [Name] and all who believe in you.
We ask this through our Lord Jesus Christ,
your Son, who lives and reigns with you and
the Holy Spirit, one God, forever and ever.
Amen.

ACT TOGETHER

Taking a cue from the story of Venerable Pierre Toussaint, discuss ways that you can be of generous service to others in your family or community. Decide on one specific action you can take together to share your time or talent with others.

Your Plan Write about the action you chose:

BEING CATHOLIC

Together: Explore these poems by famous Catholics and discuss what they describe about the Holy Spirit.

Oh, morning, at the brown brink eastward, springs—
Because the Holy Ghost over the bent
World broods with warm breast and with ah! bright wings.

—From *God's Grandeur* by Gerard Manley Hopkins

The Spirit of God / is a life that bestows life, / root of the world-tree / and wind in its boughs. / Scrubbing out sins, / she rubs oil into wounds.

—From *Antiphon for the Holy Spirit* by Hildegard of Bingen

Faith Walk

Spiritual companioning Talk about the story in **Journeys Today.**

- Identify persons or times related to spiritual companioning from which either of you have benefited.
- Investigate the opportunities provided at your local parish for faith-sharing groups.

Together: Reflect on your own experience of the Holy Spirit.

- How do you imagine the Holy Spirit?
- When or how are you aware of the Holy Spirit?
- Which titles of the Holy Spirit are most significant to you?

Empowered by the Spirit

I would like your blessing. Depending on the situation, these words might infer different things. They might be a request for someone's approval, or they might be a request for a go-ahead.

What a blessing! We hear these words when something good happens—either miraculous or just plain lucky.

God bless you. Sometimes these words are an automatic response when someone sneezes. At other times, they are said from the heart to wish someone something special.

- **What does *blessing* mean for you?**
- **Recall a significant blessing that was part of your life experience.**

Gathering Rite

Procession with the Word

Sing together.

Go make a difference.
We can make a difference.
Go make a difference in the world.

"Go Make a Difference," © 1997, Steve Angrisano and Thomas N. Tomaszek. Published by spiritandsong.com®

Leader: Let us pray.

All: *Pray the Sign of the Cross together.*

Leader: We gather together to give praise and thanks for the gift of the Holy Spirit who lives in us and empowers us with abundant goodness and blessings.

All: Amen.

Leader: Lord, make us open to the fullness of the Gifts and Fruits of your Holy Spirit, that we may be signs of your presence and messengers of your Good News. We ask this through Jesus Christ our Lord.

All: Amen.

Celebration of the Word

Leader: A reading from the Book of the prophet Isaiah.
Read Isaiah 11:1–5.
The word of the Lord.

All: Thanks be to God.

Reflect silently.

What Gifts of the Holy Spirit do you most want for yourself?

RITUAL FOCUS

Blessing of Candidates

Come forward as directed. Leader places hands on each candidate's head, makes the Sign of the Cross, and prays.

Leader: [Name], in Baptism you received the gifts of faith and new life in Christ. We pray for God's blessing on you as you prepare to share more fully in this life through the Gifts of the Holy Spirit.

Candidate: Amen.

General Intercessions

Leader: Let us pray.

Reader 1: For the gift of wisdom for ourselves, for the Church, and for world leaders, we pray to the Lord.

All: Come, Holy Spirit.

Reader 2: For the gift of understanding that we may come to know the meaning of God's action and presence in our lives. For the gift of right judgment that we will make choices that will lead us to grow as his children, we pray to the Lord.

All: Come, Holy Spirit.

Reader 3: For the gift of courage to live as true disciples of Jesus. For the gift of knowledge to see our lives through God's eyes, we pray to the Lord.

All: Come, Holy Spirit.

Reader 4: For the gift of reverence to love and worship God and respect all of his creation. For the gift of wonder and awe to recognize how great God is, we pray to the Lord.

All: Come, Holy Spirit.

Leader: Let us pray as Jesus has taught us.

Pray the Lord's Prayer together.

Going Forth

Leader: Loving Father, we pray for the Gifts of the Holy Spirit that we may be witnesses of your Son, Jesus. We ask this through Christ our Lord.

All: Amen.

Sing again the opening song.

Celebrate

Gifts of the Spirit

Reflect

on the Celebration

Your Confirmation Reflections

*What thoughts did this celebration raise about becoming a confirmed Catholic?

*Which of God's blessings would help you "share more fully" in your faith journey?

*What did participating in the celebration teach you about Jesus, the Holy Spirit, or the Church?

Faith Sharing

With a partner or in a small group, reread the General Intercessions. Choose one of them and together identify people you know who exhibit each of the Gifts of the Spirit named in the intercession. Following your catechist's directions, create a "who is" game to be played with the larger group.

SIGNS OF FAITH

Blessing The Scriptures give clues to a variety of meanings for the word and action of blessing.

- It is about praise. (See *Psalm 33:1.*)
- It expresses a wish or desire that good fortune, especially of a spiritual or supernatural kind, will be with a person or thing. (See *Psalm 128:1–2.*)
- It points to the sanctification or dedication of a person or thing to some sacred purpose. (See *Matthew 26:26.*)
- It is used to designate a gift. (See *2 Kings 6:15.*)

Gestures and prayers of blessing place the person or object under God's care. God is the source of all our blessings because God is the source of all goodness and favor. Blessings, which are *sacramentals* or signs of God's presence, have been used as a form of prayer since Old Testament times.

Liturgical blessings use a set formula and are given by a priest or bishop. Simple blessings are made with prayer and the Sign of the Cross. They may be given by lay people.

Read the Scripture passages cited above. Which of the meanings expressed in the passage are significant to you?

What did the experience of being blessed and prayed for during the celebration mean for you?

Giver of Gifts

The Gifts of the Holy Spirit are first given to us at Baptism. Confirmation increases these Gifts, which are both powers and inclinations to act in ways that help us grow in our relationship to Jesus, God's Son. They give us the help to lead an active Christian life in the world. They also help us know and do God's will. But the help the Gifts of the Holy Spirit offer us is not automatic. Just as material gifts need to be opened and used to be appreciated and effective, so also the Gifts of the Holy Spirit need to be opened and used over and over again.

All-powerful God, Father of our Lord Jesus Christ
by water and the Holy Spirit
you freed your sons and daughters from sin
and gave them new life.
Send your Holy Spirit upon them
to be their Helper and Guide.
Give them the spirit of wisdom and understanding,
the spirit of right judgment and courage,
the spirit of knowledge and reverence.
Fill them with the spirit of wonder and awe in your presence.
We ask this through Christ our Lord.
Amen.

Rite of Confirmation, 25

REFLECT

Sometimes people write the following phrase on wedding or birthday invitations: *No presents. Your presence is gift enough.* How would you feel if that message were on your next birthday or high school graduation invitation? What does that phrase say about giving or receiving gifts?

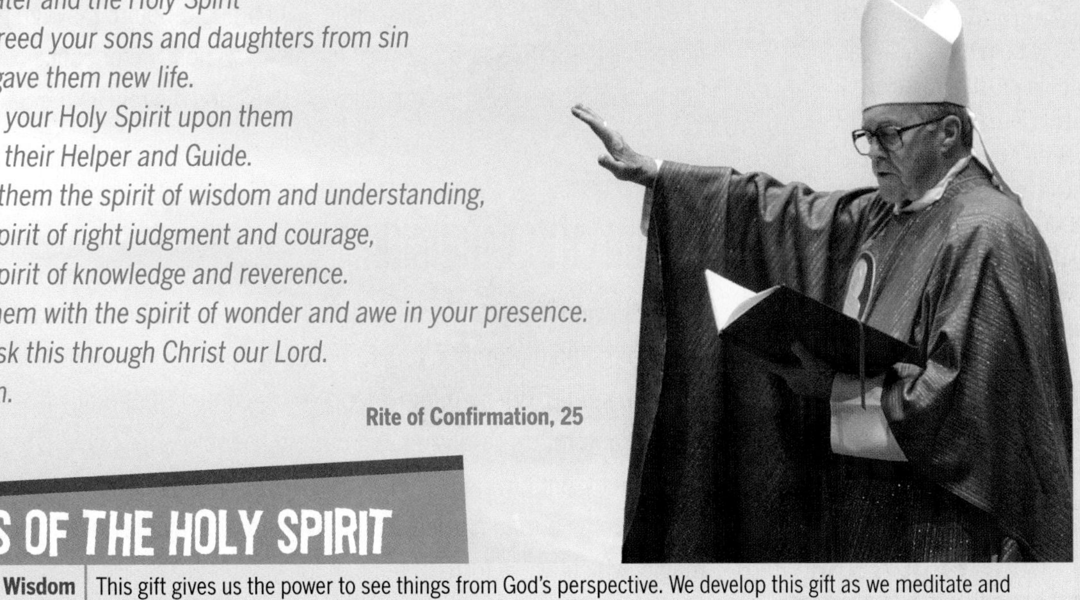

GIFTS OF THE HOLY SPIRIT

Wisdom	This gift gives us the power to see things from God's perspective. We develop this gift as we meditate and contemplate God's presence, action, and guidance in our lives. This kind of reflection helps us clarify what we believe and guides us to make right judgments and good decisions. It is the power to love what is of God.
Understanding	This gift gives us a way to understand the Tradition of the Church. It helps us get to the heart of revealed truth even when we do not fully understand its entire meaning. It gives us confidence in the revealed word of God and leads us to draw orthodox conclusions from the Scriptures and doctrine. It is the power to know how to live as followers of Jesus and apply the teachings of the Church to daily life.
Right Judgment	This gift helps us know what we should do in difficult situations. It helps us correctly judge our actions. It is the power to know how to make right choices and good decisions.
Courage	This gift ensures a confident spirit of resolution, firmness of mind, and strong will to persevere, knowing that God's providence will enable us to overcome all obstacles. It helps us persist in the practice of virtue even when we fail or are persecuted for trying. It is the power to stand up for our beliefs and the values of Jesus' message even when it is difficult.
Knowledge	This gift enables us to judge what is happening in relationships, the environment, and social situations. We are able to see God's providence in what happens in our lives. Those who have knowledge can distinguish between impulses and the inspirations of grace. It is the power to see all of life and creation through God's eyes.
Reverence	This gift places us in a right relationship with God. It enables us to see God as a loving Father. Pope John Paul II described it as a gift that opens our hearts to "tenderness towards God and our brothers and sisters . . . expressed in prayer." It is the power to see God's presence in all people and life experiences.
Wonder and Awe	This gift inspires us with awareness of God's majesty and the fact that he has created us in his image. Through it we know that we have a spiritual dimension and live in relationship with God. It is the power to recognize how awesome God truly is.

Gifts for Mission

SCRIPTURE BACKGROUND

Samaria was the capital of the northern kingdom of Israel for most of its existence. It was viewed as corrupt because of the indifference of the wealthy to those who were poor and because there was a certain heterodoxy of religion, which included idolatry and false worship. (See *Kings 17:29.*) It is probably from these religious roots that Simon, the Magician, practiced his form of magic as a religion. In the New Testament, Jesus reaches out to the Samaritans. (See *Luke 10:29–37, Luke 17:11–19, John 4:1–42.*) In Acts, Philip, the deacon, with the approval of the church in Jerusalem, becomes the evangelizer of the Samaritans through his preaching and signs and wonders.

FAITH FOCUS

Why does God give us gifts?

What a difference the Gifts of the Holy Spirit made in Peter and the other Apostles. After the Holy Spirit descended upon them at Pentecost, they were strengthened to build up the Church in Jerusalem. They were given the power to heal and to preach about Jesus' Resurrection without any fear!

During Jesus' passion and death, Peter denied knowing Jesus. However, after Pentecost when Peter and John were brought before the high priest and questioned about their preaching and ability to heal, Peter spoke out very boldly about the Resurrection of Jesus Christ and his role as the Savior.

Holy Land

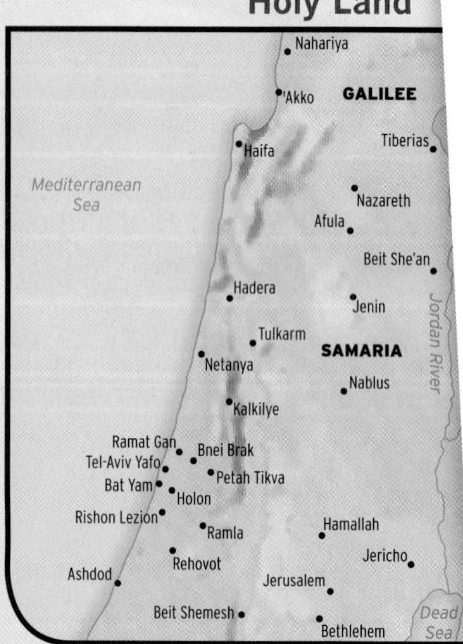

Simon, the Magician

Philip went down to Samaria and proclaimed the Messiah to them. The crowds paid attention to him because they saw the signs he was doing. Unclean spirits, crying out in a loud voice, came out of many possessed people; and many paralyzed and crippled people were cured. There was great joy in that city.

There was a man named Simon living in the city. He used to practice magic, which was a form of religion for many pagans. He was highly thought of by his followers who called him "Power of God." However, when his followers began to follow Philip, even Simon came to believe. He was baptized and became a follower and was astounded by the signs and wonders that were occurring.

When the Apostles in Jerusalem heard that Samaria had accepted the word of God, they sent them Peter and John, who went down and prayed for them that they might receive the Holy Spirit. Then they laid hands on them and they received the Holy Spirit.

When Simon saw that the Spirit was conferred by the laying on of hands, he offered them money and said, "Give me also this power so that anyone on whom I lay my hands may receive the Holy Spirit." But Peter said to him, "May your silver perish with you, because you thought you could obtain God's gift with money! You have no part or share in this, for your heart is not right before God."

Based on Acts 8:4–21

What was Simon's dilemma?

How has or will the Gift of the Spirit enhance your life?

The Gifts of the Holy Spirit are not given to us just for our personal relationship with Jesus. They are gifts that are meant to be shared with others and used for the benefit of the Church and its mission to bring the Good News to others.

REFLECT

Think about gifts you have received. Which ones did you want to keep just for yourself? Which ones did you want to share with others?

Spiritual Gifts

Now there are varieties of gifts, but the same Spirit;
and there are varieties of services, but the same Lord;
and there are varieties of activities, but it is the same God
who activates all of them in everyone. To each is given
the manifestation of the Spirit for the common good.

—1 Corinthians 12:4–7

Each of us is given gifts that we use all the time, but we may not always be aware of them as spiritual gifts. Some of us can teach. We may use that gift very intentionally by tutoring or coaching others. Some of us have the gift of visualizing and vocalizing. We see injustice and need and we are able to speak up about what we see and feel even when it is unpopular to do that. Our speaking up often leads us and others to act on behalf of the needy and more vulnerable people in our midst. Some of us are naturally healers and forgivers. We are able, through our words and actions, to bring healing and forgiveness to others or to create peace in situations that are fractured or volatile. When we use our spiritual gifts for others, we participate in building the common good.

Share the Word

In the story from Acts, Philip, James, and John each use different gifts or powers to build up the church in Samaria.

- Identify which gift each of them used.
- Reflect on how you do or could use the Gifts of the Holy Spirit for the common good of the significant communities in your life (family, friends, school, work).
- With a partner, share an insight you have about your own sharing of gifts for the common good.

Conversion

REFLECT

What images or words does the word *conversion* elicit in you?

DISCUSS

Recall and describe an experience of conversion that you have observed in someone else.

FAITH FOCUS

How are we called to use the Gifts of the Holy Spirit?

During the Confirmation celebration, the bishop will speak about the first Pentecost. He will remind you that you first received the Holy Spirit at Baptism. He will also urge you to live in a way that others will see God's goodness in you. In his own words, he will say:

> *You must be witnesses before all the world to his suffering, death, and resurrection; your way of life should at all times reflect the goodness of Christ. Christ gives varied gifts to his Church, and the Spirit distributes them among the members of Christ's Body to build up the holy people of God in unity and love.*
>
> **Rite of Confirmation, 22**

A change

Committing yourself to being a "witness to all the world" may require some changes for you. *Conversion* means to change—to move away from doing or being one way to doing or being another way. Spiritual conversion involves being sorry for our sins and wanting to change our ways and turn toward God. Conversion can be a big change or it can be a small one. On our faith journey, there are many moments of conversion, or times when we turn more toward being and acting as disciples or followers of Jesus. Some examples of conversions are the following:

- moving from being impatient with younger siblings to being more patient
- moving from praying very little to setting aside time for prayer every day
- moving from using your time for all the activities you want to do for yourself to volunteering time for others
- moving from spending all your money on yourself to sharing it with those in need

The most important thing to remember about conversion is that it is a process of becoming united more closely to Jesus and growing more like him. The seven Gifts of the Holy Spirit help us on that journey when we use them.

Using the Gifts of the Spirit

The Gifts of the Holy Spirit call us to be responsible members of the Church and to help others come to know and love Jesus and his Church.

We are not disciples of Jesus alone. We share the faith of the Church as a whole and as our local parish community. We depend on one another for support in our faith, for prayer, for guidance, and for good example. Our parish communities depend on our participation in other ways too. Parishes need young people involved in liturgy, helping out with service projects, and participating in faith-sharing groups and religious education sessions.

Evangelization

We are also responsible to *evangelize* or bring the Good News of Jesus to others. In order to evangelize, people need to know Jesus and have a good relationship with him. Then evangelization becomes easier, because when you have a good relationship with Jesus, you will want to share it with others.

You evangelize when you talk to others about how important your faith is, or when you consciously use your gifts to take care of the poor and needy, or when you work for justice. You evangelize when you try to live out the call to holiness you first received in Baptism. Evangelization can be done in your home, in the hallways, on the athletic field, in your school, and in your neighborhood.

CATHOLIC SOURCES

***Redemptoris Missio*, "The Mission of Christ the Redeemer,"** was Pope John Paul II's eighth encyclical. It emphasizes the importance of missionary evangelization, examines the question and opportunity for missionary activity in modern cities, and states that some traditionally Christian areas need re-evangelization. At the same time it emphasizes the continued importance of a mission to the nations. Pope John Paul's encyclical rejects any views of salvation and mission that would focus on humanity's earthly needs without being open to the "transcendent."

SYMBOL OF THE HOLY SPIRIT

Fire Have you ever heard these words: "Somebody needs to light a fire under you"? Such a statement indicates that you need energizing, inspiration, or motivation. Fire is an apt symbol of the Holy Spirit because that is what the Holy Spirit does in us. Fire purifies, warms, and gives light. It symbolizes the transforming energy of the Spirit. John the Baptist proclaimed that Jesus would "baptize you with the Holy Spirit and fire" (*Luke 3:16*). Jesus came "to bring fire to the earth" (*Luke 12:49*) and, on Pentecost, the Spirit came in the form of tongues "as of fire" (*Acts 2:3–4*). Paul also uses the image saying, "Do not quench the Spirit" (*1 Thessalonians 5:19*).

In what ways does this symbol of the Holy Spirit apply to your faith journey as you prepare for Confirmation?

Witnesses of Faith

Journeys Past

Kateri Tekakwitha, Lily of the Mohawks (1656–1680)

1656 She is born in a Mohawk village in Auriesville, New York, to a Christian Algonquin mother and a non-Christian father, who is a Mohawk chief.

1660 Her parents and brother die of smallpox, leaving her an orphan. As a result of the epidemic, she is disfigured and partially blind, so she is called Tekakwitha, which means "one who walks groping for her way." Poetically, her name is translated as "one who puts everything in order." She goes to live with her aunts and an uncle who was a Mohawk chief of the Turtle clan.

1667 At age 10, Kateri learns about Jesus from the Jesuit missionaries who spend three days in her uncle's lodge. Although she is a believer and begins to live as a follower of Jesus, she does not ask to be baptized yet. Because the members of the Turtle clan are non-Christian, her faith is put to many tests.

1676 Tekakwitha is baptized and receives the name Kateri (Catherine) on Easter Sunday.

1677 Kateri escapes to a Christian village in Quebec, where she lives in the cabin of Anastasia Tegonhatsihonga, another Christian Native American woman. Kateri is well liked in her new village because of her kindness and her cheerful willingness to help look after the children and aid the sick.

1680 She dies at the age of 24.

1943 She is declared Venerable by Pope Pius XII.

1980 Kateri is the first Native American and first American laywoman declared to be Blessed by Pope John Paul II.

"Who can tell me what is most pleasing to God that I may do it?"

Patroness of Environment and Ecology
also known as the evangelizer of Native Americans

Your Journey

Care for God's Creation

Faith in Action

Isaiah describes God's kingdom as a beloved community of all God's creatures. Every creature, every species is precious to our Creator. But species are being made extinct and the world's resources are being gobbled up with little thought of future generations. Like Blessed Kateri Tekakwitha and other Native Americans, we can adopt a new attitude toward the earth as a community to which we belong, not as a commodity belonging to us. Besides recycling more and driving less, youth can join with groups like the Natural Resources Defense Council to defend endangered species and protect a portion of the world's rainforests through the Rainforest Action Network.

Visit **www.harcourtreligion.com** to discover more about Catholic social teachings.

Journeys Today

Living Witness

When I was a child, I used to garden with my dad. He taught me that there was a natural rhythm to the earth. We never used pesticides or chemicals. And from the beginning of my life, I saw that the earth is self-sustaining without artificial things. I have always loved to see the change of the seasons and the rhythm of the earth.

Nature is the best place for me to pray. I meditate in my garden. When I go for a walk or run and see the beauty of creation, I pray in praise and thanksgiving.

My interest in a pure and safe environment became more focused when my daughter was born. I began to research foods and fabrics and gradually I began to eat organic foods and wear organic clothes. I was introduced to environmentally aware companies and was led to start my own business, where we provide naturally made clothing at reasonable prices.

Through the process of doing all this, I have found my life work: to be a steward of the earth. What started out as something for myself and my family has gradually called me to care about and respect and advocate for others—especially for workers on farms and in factories who live and work in unsafe environments. I believe God wants us to make choices that will leave the earth better not worse for those who will come after us.

Courtney F.

Meditation

Faith Walk

Christian meditation is a form of quiet contemplation often associated with prayer or Scripture study. Formal Christian meditation began with the early Christian monastic practice of reading the Bible slowly. Monks would carefully consider the deeper meaning of each verse as they read it. This slow and thoughtful reading of Scripture, and the ensuing pondering of its meaning, was their meditation. This spiritual practice is called "divine reading," or *lectio divina.* To practice this form of meditation, find a quiet place where you will not be distracted, Quiet yourself by breathing deeply. Choose a Scripture passage and read it slowly. Focus your attention on a word or phrase. Reflect on it for a time. Reread the passage. Reflect on how the passage applies to you.

Respond in Faith

Your Confirmation Reflections

*In what ways do you want to be empowered?

*Which Gifts of the Spirit most intrigue you and why?

*Which parts of the stories of Kateri and Courtney most resonate with your life?

Faith Sharing

In small groups discuss the part of this session that

- most interested you
- most challenged you

Spend some time in group silence thinking about what this session is calling you to change or strengthen in your relationship with God, yourself, or others. At the appropriate time, share this with the group.

Closing Prayer

**All powerful and living Father,
Pour out your Holy Spirit on us that we may be strengthened
to live out the call of our Baptism.
Open us to be responsive to the Gifts of the Holy Spirit
that we may grow in knowledge and love of your Son, Jesus,
become messengers of the Good News,
and further your kingdom here on earth.
We ask this in the name of Jesus Christ, who is Lord.
Amen.**

Respond in Faith Together

FAITH FOCUS

Discuss the following beliefs together. Focus on how these beliefs have or could have an effect on your lives today. Refer to the lesson if necessary.

- We receive the Gifts of the Holy Spirit at Confirmation.
- These gifts are helps, powers, and inclinations to act in ways that will help us grow in our relationship to Jesus, the Son of God, and benefit the community.
- Christian conversion is a movement toward being and acting as disciples or followers of Jesus.

RITUAL FOCUS

Read together the text on Blessing on page 46. At the end of your time together, each of you should offer a spontaneous prayer of blessing for the other.

ACT TOGETHER

Decide on an activity you can do together where each of you uses your gifts for the benefit of others. Check to see if it can be a part of your service project.

Suggestions:

- Volunteer to help in a parish activity.
- Prepare a meal for someone who is homebound.
- Do a Scripture reading and have a discussion at a family meal.

Your Plan Write about the activity or service project you chose:

BEING CATHOLIC

Together: Discuss these quotes from famous Catholics. Focus on how they apply to your life.

"Be kind and merciful. Let no one ever come to you without coming away better and happier. Be the loving expression of God's kindness."

— **Blessed Mother Teresa**

"Never be in a hurry; do everything quietly and in a calm spirit. Do not lose your inner peace for anything whatsoever, even if your whole world seems upset."

— **Saint Francis de Sales**

"The proof of love is in the works."

— **Pope Saint Gregory the Great**

Faith Walk

Meditation Talk about the story in **Journeys Today.**

- Identify times or situations that might open up opportunities for meditation for either of you.
- Discuss how meditation can help you feel closer to God.

Together: Reflect on how you have experienced the Gifts of the Holy Spirit in your life. Think of an experience of conversion in your life and share it.

Anointed by the Spirit

It's been sealed off.

Depending on the situation, these words might mean different things. They might indicate closure, safety, or untouchability.

Let's seal the deal.

We hear these words when two or more parties have communicated and negotiated a common agreement they promise to honor.

"Set me as a seal upon your heart." *(Song of Solomon 8:6)*

This reading is often used at wedding liturgies to mirror the significance and interplay of interpersonal love and loyalty.

- **What does being anointed or sealed mean for you?**
- **Recall an experience in which being sealed, anointed, or set apart was significant for you.**

Gathering Rite

Procession with the Word

Sing together.

Your Spirit, O God, is upon me,
you have anointed me.

"You Have Anointed Me," © 1981, Damean Music

Leader: Let us pray.

All: *Pray the Sign of the Cross together.*

Leader: God, our Father, you sent Jesus to bring us the Good News. May we recognize the power of anointing and come to know that we are called to continue to serve those in need. May we always praise you, your Son, Jesus, and the Holy Spirit, who lives and reigns forever and ever.

All: Amen.

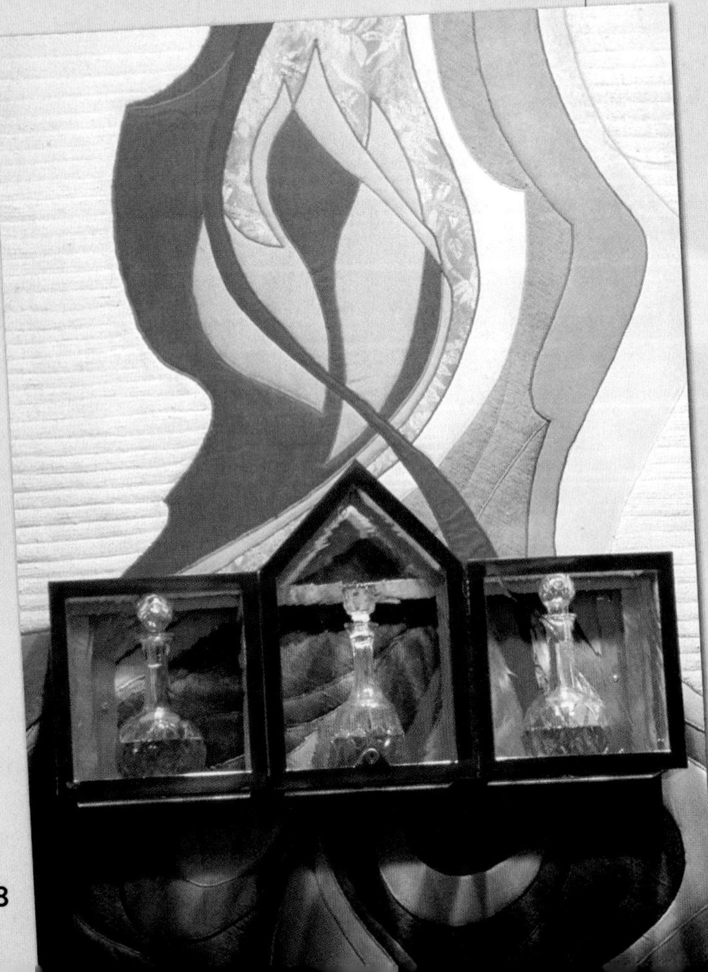

Celebration of the Word

Leader: A reading from the Book of the prophet Isaiah.
Read Isaiah 61:1–3, 6, 8–9.
The word of the Lord.

All: Thanks be to God.

Reflect silently.

What does being a part of "a people blessed by God" mean for you as you prepare for Confirmation?

RITUAL FOCUS

Procession with Oils

Leader: During Holy Week, our parish community received from (Arch)Bishop [Name] the holy oils blessed and consecrated for the sacramental life of the community.

The oil of the sick.

The oil of the sick is brought forward.
Sing a verse of the opening song.

By laying on of hands and anointing with this oil, and with the prayerful support of this community, may those who are sick experience the healing presence of Christ.

The oil of catechumens.

The oil of catechumens is brought forward.
Sing a verse of the opening song.

Anointed with this oil and assisted by this community's example, may our catechumens persevere in their journey to the saving waters of Baptism and share in Christ's victory over sin and the power of evil.

The oil of chrism.

The oil of chrism is brought forward. Sing a verse of the opening song.

Through the anointing with chrism, may all who are baptized and confirmed, all who are ordained to the service of God's people, and the parish assembly whose altar and church are dedicated to God's glory, fill the world with the sweet fragrance of Christ's Gospel and be built up as living stones into a temple filled with the Holy Spirit.

Let us pray as Jesus has taught us.

Pray the Lord's Prayer together.

Going Forth

Leader: Let us pray.

God, our Father, let the Holy Spirit you sent to your Church anoint and seal us that we may preach the Gospel and continue your work in the world. We ask this through our Lord Jesus Christ, your Son, who lives and reigns with you and the Holy Spirit, one God, forever and ever.

All: Amen.

Sing again the opening song.

Holy Oil

Reflect

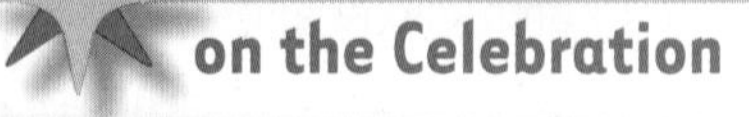

on the Celebration

Your Confirmation Reflections

*What thoughts did the celebration raise for you about being anointed?

*How were you affected by the procession with oils?

*Think of all the ways you use oil. Choose one of them and write about any similarities to the way oil is used at Confirmation.

Faith Sharing

With a partner or in a small group, come up with a statement about what being anointed with the holy oil of chrism might mean for young people being confirmed today.

SIGNS OF FAITH

Sacramentals Actions, sacred signs, or objects that are blessed by the Church and help people pray or think of God are called *sacramentals*. Sacramentals such as holy water, medals, statues, holy oils, blessings, or incense are not sacraments because they were instituted by the Church, not Christ. They also do not give grace like sacraments do. But they help a person respond to the grace received in the sacraments and lead a person to devotion, prayer, faith, and charity. Blessings are among the most important sacramentals. In blessings we praise God for his works and gifts and pray that we and others will use God's gifts in ways that reflect the Gospel message.

Name one sacramental you have used or have seen someone else use. Explain how it might lead a person to devotion, prayer, faith, or charity.

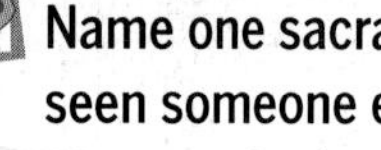

Anointing

The holy oils used in the celebration of sacraments are signs of the power and presence of the Holy Spirit. A bishop blesses the oil of catechumens and the oil of the sick, and consecrates the holy chrism, usually on Holy Thursday, at a special Mass called the Chrism Mass. Then each local parish receives a supply of these oils.

- The oil of the sick is used to anoint those who are sick.
- The oil of catechumens is used to anoint catechumens who are being accepted into the Church to strengthen them on their journey of faith. It is also used to anoint infants and young children before the Rite of Baptism.
- Chrism is a combination of olive oil and balsam. It signifies abundance of grace and committed service to God. Chrism is used in several sacraments: Baptism, Confirmation, and Holy Orders.

After the Baptism of an infant or a young child, the priest or deacon anoints his or her head with chrism. During Confirmation the bishop anoints the forehead of the person being confirmed with chrism. This second anointing, given by the bishop, confirms and completes the anointing at Baptism. Chrism is also used in the ordination of bishops and priests. It is also used to consecrate a new altar.

DISCUSS

With a partner or in a small group, brainstorm the sights, smells, sounds, or tastes that come to mind when you reflect on the word *oil*.

Anointed with the Spirit

SCRIPTURE BACKGROUND

Saul and David David is the most well-known and loved of all the kings of Israel, but he was not the first king. Saul was. Saul showed great promise when he was chosen and anointed. However, he disobeyed God and would not acknowledge that Yahweh was truly the king and he was the servant. So Saul was replaced by David who, in the beginning, did not show much royal potential. In spite of his many weaknesses and sins, he continued to love and trust God and deepen his relationship with him, thus becoming a great king.

FAITH FOCUS

What does the Rite of Anointing signify?

Anointing with oil is an ancient ritual. It was used in both religious and civil ceremonies as a symbolic action. It set the one who was anointed apart for special service. We can find stories of anointing throughout the Scriptures. We read that Samuel, who was the last of the Judges, anointed Saul as first king of the Israelites.

Anointing of Saul

"Tell the boy to go on before us, and when he has passed on, stop here yourself for a while, that I may make known to you the word of God." Samuel took a vial of oil and poured it on his head, and kissed him; he said, "The Lord has anointed you ruler over his people Israel. You shall reign over the people of the Lord and you will save them from the hand of their enemies all around."

—1 Samuel 9:27–10:1

However, Saul was not a good king. He turned away from following God and did not carry out his commands. Because he rejected God and his commands, God sent Samuel to Bethlehem to search out another king from the sons of Jesse.

 **What does God's rejection of Saul tell you about being anointed or chosen?**

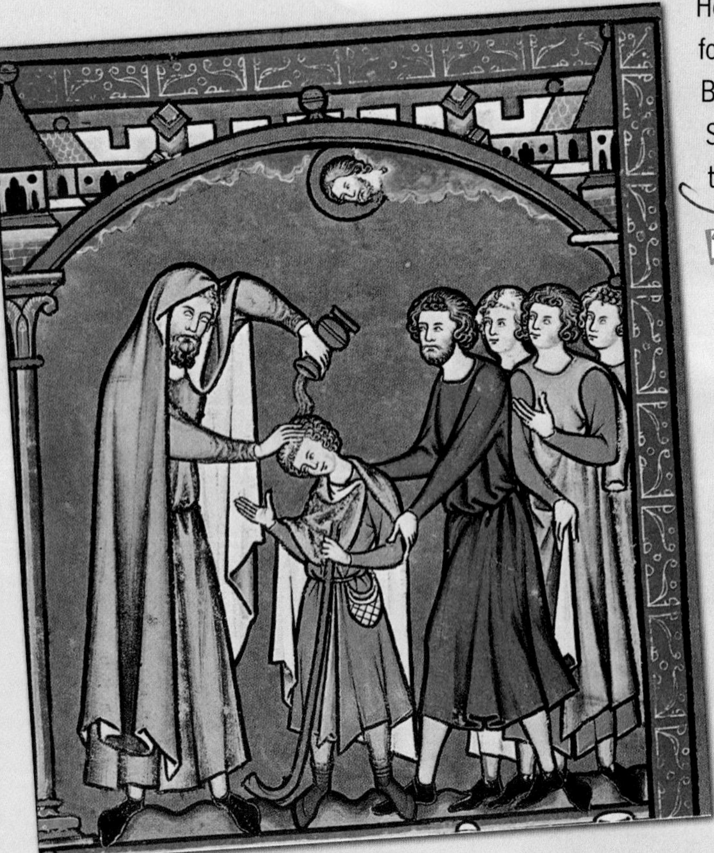

David Annointed by Samuel
French manuscript illumination (c. 1250)

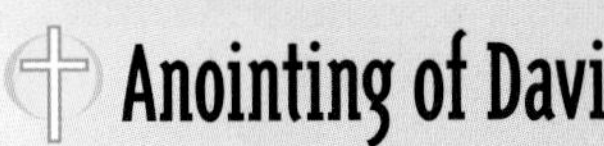

Anointing of David

> **REFLECT**
> **How do you feel about being *set apart* by the anointing at Confirmation?**

The Lord *said to Samuel, "How long will you grieve over Saul? I have rejected him from being king over Israel. Fill your horn with oil and set out; I will send you to Jesse the Bethlehemite, for I have provided for myself a king among his sons." . . . Samuel did what the* Lord *commanded, and came to Bethlehem.*

—1 Samuel 16:1, 4

There he met seven of Jesse's sons but none of them was God's choice for King.

Why does God tell Samuel to fill his horn with oil?

Samuel realized that the Lord had not chosen any of the seven sons and asked Jesse if he had more. Jesse replied that there was one more, his youngest son, David, who was tending sheep. When David was brought before him, the Lord said:

"Rise and anoint him; for this is the one." Then Samuel took the horn of oil, and anointed him in the presence of his brothers and the spirit of the Lord *came mightily upon David from that day forward.*

—1 Samuel 16:12–13

What would it mean for a young person today if the Spirit of the Lord *came mightily* upon him or her?

Anointing of Jesus

When Peter tells the Good News about Jesus to the Gentiles in Caesarea, he speaks of Jesus' anointing:

"God anointed Jesus of Nazareth with the Holy Spirit and with power; how he went about doing good and healing all who were oppressed by the devil, for God was with him."

—Acts 10:38

How does the power of the Spirit affect your actions?

Share the Word

Psalm 23 is a song David wrote after he was anointed. It describes his relationship with God.

- Read the psalm silently.
- Put into your own words the meaning conveyed by the psalm.
- Using your words, create a poem or rap to share this message.

Sealed with the Spirit

DISCUSS
With a partner or in a small group, brainstorm the gifts and responsibilities of someone who is sealed with the Spirit.

FAITH FOCUS

What does it mean to be sealed with the Spirit?

In the celebration of sacraments and in blessings, anointing with oil is always a sign of the presence of the Holy Spirit. In Baptism the anointing with chrism brings together the newly baptized with Christ who is priest, prophet, and king. Both the terms *Messiah* and *Christ* mean "Anointed One." Sometimes we say the baptized person is *christened*. He or she is now a *Christian*.

The anointing with the oil of chrism—along with the laying on of hands and the words "Be sealed with the Gift of the Holy Spirit"—is the essential sacramental sign of Confirmation. Through this anointing, we receive a spiritual character and the indelible "mark" or seal of the Holy Spirit. This anointing marks us as belonging completely to Christ. Because of this, we share fully in his mission to preach the Good News in our words and actions.

Discipleship and Mission

When we are anointed and sealed with the Holy Spirit in the Sacrament of Confirmation, we are given both gifts and responsibilities for discipleship and mission. A *disciple* is both a believer and a student. The responsibilities of discipleship include coming to know Jesus more fully through

- reading and thinking about the Scriptures
- praying
- celebrating the sacraments
- learning from fellow believers in the Church
- doing acts of charity and justice

When we cooperate with the Spirit at work in us, we are willing to do the work of discipleship. We take part in the mission of Jesus and the Church to reach out and bring the message of Jesus to others.

Anointing with chrism

Prayer for the Blessing of Oils and Chrism

Father, by the power of your love,
make this mixture of oil and perfume
a sign and source of your blessing.
Pour out the gifts of your Holy Spirit
on our brothers and sisters who will be
anointed with it.
Let the splendor of holiness shine on the world
from every place and thing
signed with this oil.

Rite of Blessing Oils and Chrism, Roman Missal Appendix II, 25

Through the anointing with chrism in the Sacrament of Confirmation, we receive the wonderful gift of God's choice to include us in his service and mission. During the celebration, each candidate is presented to the bishop. Either the candidate or sponsor gives the bishop, or confirming priest, the young person's name. The bishop or priest will then dip his right thumb in the chrism and make the Sign of the Cross on the forehead of the candidate saying:

Bishop: *[Name], be sealed with the gift of the Holy Spirit.*

Candidate: *Amen.*

Bishop: *Peace be with you.*

Candidate: *And also with you.*

Rite of Confirmation, 27

Mission of the Baptized In fact, the call to mission is a grace as well as a duty for every baptized person. Those who have made it the priority choice of their lives know this well. Whoever is sent in the name of the Church to proclaim the Good News is associated in a particular way with the person and mission of Jesus himself. In this regard Saint John says: "As you did send me into the world, so I have sent them into the world" (*John 17:18*). We are sent into the world by Christ!

Pope John Paul II, May 2000

SYMBOL OF THE HOLY SPIRIT

Seal In English the word *seal* means "to close; guarantee or assure; finalize or wrap up." In the Sacraments of Baptism, Confirmation, and Holy Orders, the visible anointing with chrism points to the invisible sealing of the person by and with the Holy Spirit. It also indicates the permanent effect of the Holy Spirit's presence on those who are anointed. This symbol reflects the fact that each of these sacraments bestows on the one receiving the sacrament an indelible mark called a sacramental character. For that reason, they may only be received once.

What does this symbol of the Holy Spirit mean to you as you make your faith journey?

Witnesses of Faith

Journeys Past

Dorothy Day
Servant of God
(1897–1980)

1897 Born in Brooklyn, New York, Dorothy is baptized Episcopalian, but religion is not a strong part of the family life.

1906 Her family moves into a Chicago tenement after her father loses his job and they lose their home in the San Francisco earthquake.

1913 She receives a scholarship to the University of Illinois at Urbana. She is convinced that charity is not enough; people must work to eliminate the causes of social evil.

1926 Dorothy begins instructions to become a Catholic.

1927 Her daughter Tamara is born. Dorothy becomes a Catholic.

1932 She prays that some way will open up for her to use her talents to help poor workers. She meets Peter Maurin and Catholic Worker Houses are begun.

1933 The first issue of *The Catholic Worker* is published.

1941 More than 100 Catholic Worker Houses are established.

1952 Dorothy's autobiography, *The Long Loneliness*, is published.

1955 She becomes a Benedictine lay oblate.

1963 *Loaves and Fishes*, the story of the Catholic Worker Movement is published.

1980 Dorothy dies.

2000 The Vatican declares Dorothy a "Servant of God." The Archdiocese of New York opens the process for canonization.

"The greatest challenge of the day is: how to bring about a revolution of the heart."

Your Journey

Dignity of Work and the Rights of Workers

Faith in Action

Isaiah provided the vision and Dorothy Day, Servant of God, provided the example. Anointed by God's Spirit, we are sent to bring Good News to the oppressed and freedom for prisoners. Advocating for jobs with a living wage for ex-prisoners and minimum-wage workers through groups like Jobs with Justice and the Living Wage Campaign are good ways to do this. Isaiah said that God's people would rebuild cities and hire foreigners to help. Dorothy Day welcomed immigrants and opposed war in part because it destroyed cities and wasted billions of dollars that should have gone toward rebuilding cities and providing meaningful work for all. Advocate for a generous immigration policy and an end to war.

Visit **www.harcourtreligion.com** to discover more about Catholic social teachings.

Journeys Today

Living Witness

When I was a teenager, I came to the States from Mexico to help my widowed mother who was working 16-hour days at a clothing factory to support my two younger sisters and me. I worked as a dishwasher and cook. There I realized how restaurant workers suffered. My frustration with low wages and poor working conditions grew.

After the September 11th terrorist attacks, I was teaching a math class at the GED center where I had learned English and gotten my own GED. It was in the same building where displaced workers from area restaurants were meeting to form a group. I felt compelled to do something with them, because I had seen so much injustice in the treatment of workers.

I joined the political committee and collected data on wages, benefits, and career opportunities. We knew that restaurant workers didn't get the minimum wage and often had to work unpaid overtime and that people of color were usually relegated to the lower-paying back-of-the-house jobs, like runner, busboy, and dish washer. But we got the actual numbers to prove it. After a full year of pressing the case with the state legislature, our efforts resulted in the passage of a bill that raised the minimum wage for hourly workers and those whose wages are dependent on tips.

I credit the example of my mother and my Catholic faith with helping me sustain my vision of a more just life.

Rafael D.

Eucharist

Faith Walk

Participation in the Eucharist each week strengthens us on the journey of faith. It is the source and summit of the Christian life. It is what forms us as Church. We are reminded as we gather as an assembly that we are God's people called to give praise and thanks for all of God's gifts to us. We are also challenged to go out from the assembly to bring the Good News to the world. When the priest or extraordinary minister hands us the Body and Blood of Jesus, we say *Amen*, or yes to that challenge. Just as food nourishes our bodies, the Eucharist strengthens our souls and deepens our charity for all of our brothers and sisters. It commits us to the poor and binds us together as the Body of Christ. We become what we eat and drink and are empowered to live for others.

Respond in Faith

Your Confirmation Reflections

If you are involved in a service project as a part of your preparation for Confirmation, develop a monthly plan for how you will continue that service or something similar for one year after Confirmation.

Choose one of the following Corporal Works of Mercy and develop a monthly plan for practicing it for one year after Confirmation.

* Feed the hungry.
* Give drink to the thirsty.
* Shelter the homeless.
* Clothe the naked.
* Visit the sick.
* Visit the imprisoned.
* Bury the dead.

Faith Sharing

In small groups discuss the part of this session that

- most interested you
- most challenged you

Spend some time in group silence thinking about what this session is calling you to change or strengthen in your relationship with God, yourself, or others. At the appropriate time, share your thoughts with the group.

closing prayer

Leader: Lord God, we wait for the pouring out of your Holy Spirit.

All: Come, Holy Spirit.

Leader: Lord God, we hope for your anointing.

All: Come, Holy Spirit.

Leader: Lord God, be with us that we may proclaim the Good News.

All: Come, Holy Spirit.

Respond in Faith Together

FAITH FOCUS

Discuss together the following beliefs. Focus on how these beliefs have or could have an effect on your lives today. Refer to the lesson, if necessary.

- The holy oils used in the celebration of sacraments are signs of the power and presence of the Holy Spirit.
- Anointing signifies being chosen and sealed with the Holy Spirit.
- In Confirmation, we are anointed for discipleship and mission.

RITUAL FOCUS

During the celebration, the candidates experienced a procession with oils. Discuss the concept of being anointed and pray together the closing prayer of the celebration on page 59.

ACT TOGETHER

Discuss the progress of the candidate's service project, if there is one. Decide on one thing you can do together to enhance the project. If there is no formal service project, refer to the action plan (page 68) the candidate is developing around one of the Works of Mercy and choose an activity you can do together.

Your Plan Write about the activity you plan to put in action:

BEING CATHOLIC

Together: Explore these quotes by famous Catholics and discuss how they relate to being anointed with the Spirit.

"The world is very different now. For man holds in his mortal hands the power to abolish all forms of human poverty, and all forms of human life."

— John F. Kennedy

"There are no hopeless situations; there are only people who have grown hopeless about them."

— Clare Boothe Luce

"I will go anywhere and do anything in order to communicate the love of Jesus to those who do not know Him or have forgotten Him."

— Saint Frances Cabrini

Faith Walk

Eucharist Talk about the story in **Journeys Today.**

- Discuss how important worship and the Eucharist are to each of you.
- Talk about the meaning of the phrase "you are what you eat."
- Reflect on how and why participating in the Eucharist leads to a commitment to those who are in need.

Together: Review the past five sessions using the following statements:

My faith has grown because . . .
I learned that you are . . .
You have helped me . . .

sanctified by the spirit

You have such spirit.

Someone might use these words because he or she has observed liveliness in another person. The speaker sees energy and passion within the person with whom they are communicating.

Team spirit is the name of the game!

When people come together with a common goal and work together to accomplish it, something happens.

His spirit was passed on to his daughter.

We often hear this when we see a member of the younger generation take up a parent's or grandparent's cause and continues to grow and develop the work.

- **What does *spirit* mean for you?**
- **Recall an experience when you or someone you know acted with a spirit inherited from someone else.**

Gathering Rite

Procession with the Word

Sing together.

Lord, have mercy.
Christ, have mercy.
Lord, have mercy.

Leader: Let us pray.

All: ***Pray the Sign of the Cross together.***

Leader: God, our Father, we give you praise and thanks for all the holy men and women of every time and place.

May they never stop interceding for us and may their prayers bring us closer to you.

We ask this through our Lord Jesus Christ, your Son, who lives and reigns with you and the Holy Spirit, one God, forever and ever.

All: Amen.

Celebration of the Word

Leader: A reading from the First Letter of John.

Read 1 John 3:1–3.

The word of the Lord.

All: Thanks be to God.

Reflect silently.

How would you apply the words "we will be like him" to yourself?

RITUAL FOCUS

Litany of Saints and Blessing with Incense

Leader: Let us ask the saints to pray for us, that we may be able to carry the light of our Baptism into the world around us.

All: ***Respond: Pray for us after each petition.***

Saint Ann and Saint Joachim

Saint Peter and Saint Paul

Saint Francis of Assisi and Saint Theresa of Lisieux

Saint Monica and Saint Augustine

Saint Perpetua and Saint Felicity

Saint Stephen and Saint Agnes

Saint Thomas Aquinas and Saint Dominic

Saint Juan Diego and Saint Rose of Lima

Add additional favorite saints names if you wish.

Leader: All you holy men and women saints of God.

All: Pray for us.

Leader: May we all grow in holiness and goodness and live after the model of Jesus, the Son of God.

All: Amen.

Leader: *Incense the group.*

All: *Bow as you are incensed.*

Leader: Let us pray as Jesus has taught us.

Pray the Lord's Prayer together.

Going Forth

Leader: Let us pray.

God, our Father, let the Spirit you sent on us in Baptism continue to renew us and make us holy that we may draw closer to you and continue your work in the world. We ask this through our Lord Jesus Christ, your Son, who lives and reigns with you and the Holy Spirit, one God, forever and ever.

All: Amen.

Sing again the opening song.

Holiness

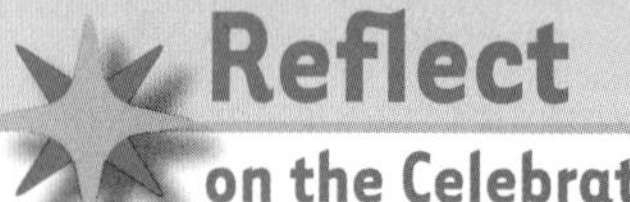

Reflect on the Celebration

Your Confirmation Reflections

*What thoughts did this celebration raise for you about holiness?

*To which part of the celebration did you pay the most attention?

*What did the celebration say to you about becoming a confirmed Catholic?

Faith Sharing

With a partner or in a small group, share who your favorite saints are and what about them is attractive to you.

- Name two important qualities of a holy person.
- In a small group, brainstorm what you think the challenges are to being a saint in the twenty-first century.

SIGNS OF FAITH

Incense One of the more important sacramentals of the Roman Catholic Church, incense is an aromatic substance that is obtained from certain resinous trees. The burning of incense creates a sacred environment. Incense is symbolic of zeal and fervor in its burning and of virtue in its fragrance. As incense rises, it reminds us of our prayers rising to God. (See *Psalm 141:2*.)

Incense also shows deep honor and reverence to the Lord and to the people and objects being incensed on special feasts and solemn occasions. Often during the celebration of the Eucharist, veneration is shown by incensing the altar and the book of the Gospels; during funerals the people and the body of the deceased are incensed. Five grains of incense are found imbedded in the Paschal Candle to signify the five wounds in Christ.

When during the Mass is incense used? What are some special times you may have seen incense used?

Holy People

Usually when we think about holy people, we do not think about ourselves or even people we know well. Instead, we think about people like Mother Teresa, Saint Francis, or one of the martyrs such as Saint Stephen. We think of people who are extraordinary witnesses of the Christian life, people with heroic virtue. We know a *saint* is a holy person who has been canonized. The Church recognizes certain people as holy through a lengthy and solemn or serious process called *canonization*. At the end of this process, the pope declares that this person has lived a life of faithfulness and is a model and witness for us.

Holiness is not reserved for canonized saints or for those who do amazing things. Everyone who is baptized is called to holiness because, in Baptism, we become a part of the Body of Christ and share in his holiness. Ordinary people who pray, who have a relationship with Jesus, who do good works, and who strive to connect their faith with their lives at home, work, school, and the larger community are holy. *Holiness* is a quality we have because we participate in God's life. God is the source of all holiness.

REFLECT

Recall persons you often come in contact with. Which ones could you call "holy"?

DISCUSS

With a partner or in a small group, discuss why it is that young people do not often think of themselves as holy or saintly.

The Sanctifier

At Baptism we are freed from sin and become part of the Church, the Body of Christ. We become members of "a chosen race, . . . a holy nation, God's own people" *(1 Peter 2:9)*. The Holy Spirit dwells in the Church and makes us a holy people. Holiness is one of the *marks of the Church*. The Holy Spirit also dwells in us. Our bodies are temples of the Holy Spirit. One of the titles of the Holy Spirit is *Sanctifier*, which means to *make holy*. On the one hand, we *are* holy through our Baptism. On the other hand, we continually *become* holy through the power of the Holy Spirit, who constantly acts in the Church and in us to make us holy and to guide us to do good and avoid what is against God's law. Confirmation increases and deepens the sense of the Holy Spirit in us. It also joins us more closely to Christ and the Church.

Christian Holiness

SCRIPTURE BACKGROUND

Synagogue The word *synagogue* means a gathering of things or an assembly of people. It refers to both a gathering of Jews and a place. There are several theories about how synagogues came to be important structures in Judaism. One theory is that the gathering of the Jewish people for fellowship, prayer, and study developed as a result of the loss of the Temple during the Babylonian captivity. Another is that synagogues developed as a resistance to assimilation into the Greek culture in the second century before Christ. However they developed, synagogues were established by the time of Jesus' public life. At that time, they were communal gathering places where marriages took place, circumcisions were performed, the Scriptures were translated aloud into Aramaic (the language of the people), town meetings were held, and the elders were consulted.

FAITH FOCUS

What does Jesus teach about holiness?

During his life on earth, Jesus showed us how to be witnesses of holiness. A *witness* is someone who gives evidence. Jesus is the best model we have of the holiness of God because he is the Son of God. Through him we learn how we are to live in relationship with God the Father and others. In the *Incarnation*, the Son of God took on a human nature and became man in order to save all people. Jesus is true God and true man, both fully divine and fully human. Because of this, he is the one and only mediator between God and humans. He is the human face of God. Jesus showed us in both words and actions what God is like.

Jesus at Nazareth

Then Jesus, filled with the power of the Spirit, returned to Galilee, and a report about him spread through all the surrounding country. He began to teach in their synagogues and was praised by everyone.

When he came to Nazareth, where he had been brought up, he went to the synagogue on the sabbath day, as was his custom. He stood up to read, and the scroll of the prophet Isaiah was given to him. He unrolled the scroll and found the place where it was written:

"The Spirit of the Lord is upon me,
because he has anointed me
to bring good news to the poor.
He has sent me to proclaim release to the captives
and recovery of sight to the blind,
to let the oppressed go free,
to proclaim the year of the Lord's favor."

And he rolled up the scroll, gave it back to the attendant, and sat down. The eyes of all in the synagogue were fixed on him. Then he began to say to them, "Today this scripture has been fulfilled in your hearing."

—Luke 4:14–19, 21

What does this Gospel tell us about holiness?

Why do you need the Holy Spirit to be a witness of holiness?

Sermon on the Mount

In an inaugural address, the president of the country lays out his vision for the country during his time of service. At the beginning of his public life, Jesus preached the Sermon on the Mount. Many people consider it his "inaugural address." It set forth the vision of his proclamation of God's reign and it gave us a blueprint for our lives as disciples. In it, Jesus teaches many things about what it means to be holy.

One of the best-known parts of this Sermon passage is the *Beatitudes*. Here Jesus identifies different behaviors or groups of people and calls them "blessed." Scripture scholars who study the original words of the Scriptures tell us that the word used for "blessed" can also mean "happy." The Beatitudes are Jesus' eight teachings about the meaning and path to true happiness; they depict the attitudes and actions that followers of Christ should have, and they reveal the way to live in God's kingdom today. They describe the way to attain the eternal holiness or blessedness to which God calls all people. When we do God's will and act in the ways of discipleship, we can find peace and happiness because we are in harmony with him.

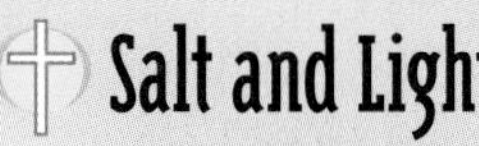

When have you experienced peace, happiness, or blessing as a result of doing God's will?

Salt and Light

Everything Jesus said and did, and all that he was, teaches us.

You are the salt of the earth; but if salt has lost its taste, how can its saltiness be restored? . . . You are the light of the world . . ., let your light shine before others, so that they may see your good works and give glory to your Father in heaven.

—Matthew 5:13, 14, 16

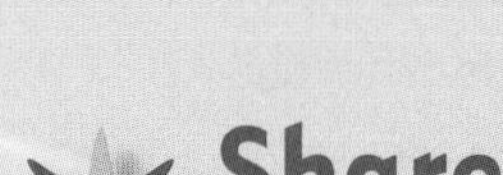

How can young people live out Jesus' command to be "salt of the earth" and "light of the world"?

REFLECT

Look up the Beatitudes in Matthew 5:3–10. Which of these Beatitudes could best describe the way you are living right now?

Share the Word

- In small groups, choose one of the three chapters of the Sermon on the Mount (*see Matthew* 5–7) and read it together.
- Discuss what messages you hear for the Christian life today.
- From the discussion, choose the one that most speaks to you and pray or write about it during the week.

Living Witnesses

DISCUSS

With a partner or in a small group, brainstorm ways that following the call to holiness might be difficult for young people.

REFLECT

There are people in your life you really like: people who know you and accept you, people who are good influences on you, people you know and enjoy spending time with. What kinds of activities helped you get to know each other? How do those friendships determine how you act? What can you do to strengthen your good friendships?

FAITH FOCUS

How do we grow in holiness?

All Christians by the example of their lives and the witness of the word, wherever they live, have an obligation to manifest the new person which they have put on in baptism, and to reveal the power of the holy Spirit by whom they were strengthened at confirmation . . .

Decree on the Church's Missionary Activity, 11

The anointing at Confirmation sanctifies us and sets us apart to be living examples of what it means to be holy. The Holy Spirit prompts or encourages us to deepen our relationship with him and the Church through prayer and actions. We grow in holiness when we follow these promptings. But it is not always easy. Sometimes we do not want to "let our light shine," especially if we believe people might think we are different or our friends and classmates might make fun of us or stop being our friends.

But Jesus does ask us to act in ways that might be difficult at times. He asks us to forgive not just once but over and over. He asks us to give to those who are in need and to love even our enemies. This can be hard. When we are faced with something difficult, we come face to face with the cross in our own lives. Being a Christian includes taking up the cross and living in the Paschal Mystery of dying to sin—to whatever keeps us from loving God and others—and rising to new life. Death and resurrection are part of every Christian's life.

Grace

We do not face our trials alone. Through Baptism we participate in the gift of life and love with God the Father, God the Son, and God the Holy Spirit. We call this participation in God's life sanctifying grace. One of the wonderful and mysterious things about God's friendship is that he initiates it. He reaches out to us. He gives us free and undeserved help to be his children, to share in his life here on earth, and to have eternal life with him in heaven. It is when we respond to his gift of grace and live in a close relationship with God the Father, God the Son, and God the Holy Spirit that we are able to do the hard things and become witnesses of God's holiness.

The Church

The Church helps us and supports us as we learn to be true disciples and grow in holiness. Through the teachings and authority of the pope and bishops, the Church's authentic teachers who are guided by the Holy Spirit, we learn what we are to believe and how we are to live as followers of Jesus. As we participate in the life of the Church, we get to know other Catholics who witness and inspire us to Christian holiness. So do the saints who have lived before us. The Church celebrates the gifts of God through the seven sacraments. Through the sacraments, especially the Eucharist, we receive the grace of the Holy Spirit who unites us more closely to Jesus, God's Son and our Savior.

CATHOLIC SOURCES

The sanctifying office of the Church The bishop and priests sanctify the Church by their prayer and work, by their ministry of the word and the sacraments. They sanctify her by their example, "not as domineering over those in your charge but by being examples to the flock." [1 Pet 5:3] Thus, "together with the flock entrusted to them, they may attain eternal life." [LG 26 § 3]

Catechism of the Catholic Church, 893

Confirmation

Confirmation strengthens the gift of sanctifying grace we received in Baptism. It unites us more fully to the Church. It gives us a special strength of the Holy Spirit to share our faith as witnesses of Christ and to never be ashamed of the cross or our faith. During the Sacrament of Confirmation, prayers are said that God will pour out his Holy Spirit so that we may be more like Christ by the way we live our lives.

Bishop:

My dear friends:
let us be one in prayer to God our Father
as we are one in faith, hope, and love his Spirit gives.

Deacon or Minister:

For these sons and daughters of God,
confirmed by the gift of the Spirit, that they give witness to Christ
by lives built of faith and love:
let us pray to the Lord.

Rite of Confirmation, 30

The Baptism of Christ, by Joachim Patinir (c. 1515)

SYMBOL OF THE HOLY SPIRIT

Dove The dove is one of the most popular symbols of the Holy Spirit. It comes from the Scriptures, which describe the baptism of Jesus when the Holy Spirit descends upon Jesus in the form of a dove and the voice of the Father proclaims that Jesus is his beloved Son. (See *Matthew 3:13–17, Mark 1:9–11, Luke 3:21–22, John 1:29–34.*) Doves are gentle birds and the use of them as a symbol points to the gentle, yet powerful, workings of the Holy Spirit. Through the Holy Spirit, we become aware of God's presence and are helped to do good. The Holy Spirit also points out our failures and nudges us in the right direction.

What are some examples of times you have been aware of the gentle presence of the Holy Spirit?

Witnesses of Faith

Journeys Past

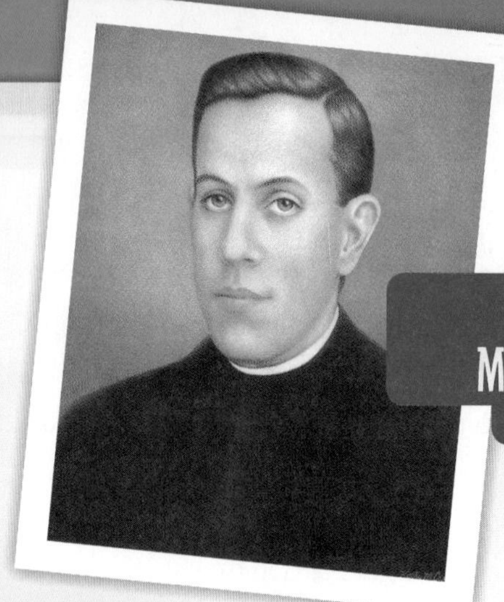

Blessed Miguel Pro (1891–1927)

1891 Miguel is born in Guadalupe, Zacatecas, Mexico. He is the third child and oldest boy in a large family. His father's position as a mine director makes him aware of the status of the workers. As a child he plans to become an engineer to help them. He is a happy child and has a devotion to Christ the King and Our Lady of Guadalupe.

1910 The Mexican Revolution begins.

1911 Miguel feels a call to the priesthood and enters the Jesuits.

1914 The political situation forces him and fellow Jesuits to leave Mexico. They are sent to Texas and later California.

1921 Miguel teaches in Nicaragua.

1925 He is ordained in Belgium.

1926 He develops stomach problems, which he tries to hide with his sense of humor. The Jesuits allow him to return to troubled Mexico. Shortly after his arrival, all public worship is forbidden by the government. But that does not stop him. He disguises himself and conducts an underground ministry, preaching the Good News in word and action. He also takes many risks collecting and distributing food and other supplies in order to help the poor of the city.

1927 Miguel is falsely accused and executed for participating in a bombing attempt.

1988 He is beatified by Pope John Paul II.

"Long live Christ the King!"

These were his last words at his execution.

Your Journey

Rights and Responsibilities of the Human Person

Faith in Action

God's holiness is love. As the Son of God, Jesus shows us what holiness/love means. His love went out especially to those "least" of his brothers and sisters. His example challenges us to accept our responsibility to be advocates for the rights of others, especially those denied these rights because of their race, gender, age, nationality, or religious background. We are to "hunger and thirst for justice," like Miguel Pro did, taking many risks collecting and distributing food and other supplies to the poor. Food is a basic human right. Bread for the World helps U.S. Christians advocate for legislation to promote this right. Invite your family, class, or parish to become a member. Write letters together.

Visit **www.harcourtreligion.com** to discover more about Catholic social teachings.

Journeys Today

Living Witness

I attended a major non-Catholic university in the midwest and became active at the Catholic Center on campus. The priests at the Center were smart, outgoing, and fantastic preachers. What they said made me think. I was impressed with how they reached out to us as students and my faith became more real and important. I think that's when the seeds were planted in my head and heart that perhaps I could do the same thing.

My senior year, I volunteered at a hospital. I spent time visiting patients in the burn unit. Sometimes I think I was able to help them answer difficult questions about life and God. Maybe this was what God was calling me to, but I wasn't sure.

As I prayed, it became clearer to me that perhaps the Holy Spirit was calling me to serve God's people as a priest. That senior year, I talked with one of the priests at the Catholic Center to gain his perspective. I decided to teach religion in a Catholic high school for one year. I prayed often about the pros and cons of becoming a priest. One day it came to me that with God's call, it was not a matter of "pros and cons" but "all or nothing." I am sure that was the Holy Spirit guiding me to know his will. So I entered the seminary and was ordained a few years later. It has been a fantastic journey.

Rev. Steven L.

Discernment

Discernment is the process of being able to grasp and understand what is obscure. Spiritual discernment is the process of grasping and understanding what God's will is in a particular or more general life situation. It involves prayer and meditation, talking to others, and paying attention to feelings and events in one's life. More than just a skill, discernment is a gift from God before it is anything else. Yet skills are clearly put to use during discernment, and people become better at it through practice. Spiritual discernment isn't usually a sudden zap from beyond, but something that emerges from the movement of the Holy Spirit and the hard work of spiritual discipline.

Faith Walk

Respond in Faith

Your Confirmation Reflections

Think about the following statements and do a self-assessment on how holy you are.

*I pray every day.

*I pray for God's guidance when I make decisions.

*I care about my friends and relate to them with care and respect.

*I am concerned about those who are poor and sick, and I reach out to them when it is appropriate.

*I feel connected to nature, and I protect it.

Faith Sharing

In small groups discuss the part of this session that

- most interested you
- most challenged you

Spend some time in group silence thinking about what this session is calling you to change or strengthen in your relationship with God, yourself, or others. At the appropriate time, share your thoughts with the group.

closing prayer

Leader: Lord God, we long to be your witnesses throughout the earth.

All: Come, Holy Spirit.

Leader: We depend on your courage and strength.

All: Come, Holy Spirit.

Leader: Make us to live always in the likeness of Jesus.

All: Come, Holy Spirit.

Respond in Faith Together

FAITH FOCUS

Discuss the following beliefs together. Focus on how these beliefs have or could have an effect on your lives today. Refer to the lesson if necessary.

- Everyone who is baptized is called to holiness because in Baptism we put on Christ.
- Jesus is the best model we have of the holiness of God.
- Being a Christian involves taking up the cross and living in the Paschal Mystery of dying to sin and rising to new life.

RITUAL FOCUS

During the celebration, the candidates experienced a Litany of the Saints and the rite of being incensed. Discuss the experience of being incensed. Share stories of your favorite saints with each other, and discuss how they are models for your own lives.

ACT TOGETHER

Read together Luke 4:14–21. Decide on an activity you can do together where you are acting on behalf of people who are poor or ill.

Suggestions:

- Contact an assisted-living facility and set up a visit with someone who does not have regular visitors.
- Accompany an extraordinary minister of Holy Communion on a Communion call.
- Contact your parish outreach committee and volunteer to assist in one of their projects for those in need.

Your Plan Write about the action you chose:

BEING CATHOLIC

Together: Explore these quotes by famous Catholics and discuss how they relate to the holiness we are called to.

"Nothing is more practical than finding God, that is, than falling in love in a quiet absolute, final way. What you are in love with, what seizes your imagination, will affect everything."

—Pedro Arrupe, S.J.

"Prayer is not so much a way to find God as a way of resting in him . . . who loves us, who is near to us. . . ."

—Thomas Merton

"We must not seek the child Jesus in the pretty figures of our Christmas cribs. We must seek him among the undernourished children who have gone to bed at night with nothing to eat . . ."

—Oscar Romero

Faith Walk

Discernment Talk about the story in **Journeys Today.**

- Discuss your experiences of discernment.
- Look over the list of the Fruits of the Holy Spirit below. Circle those that you see evident in each other. Discuss how they can be used as a discernment tool.

Charity	Kindness	Faithfulness
Joy	Goodness	Modesty
Peace	Generosity	Self-control
Patience	Gentleness	Chastity

Together: Reflect on your own feelings and thoughts about being called to holiness, considering the challenges that are raised for you in your personal and work life. Recall an experience when you have met one of those challenges.

Guided by the Spirit

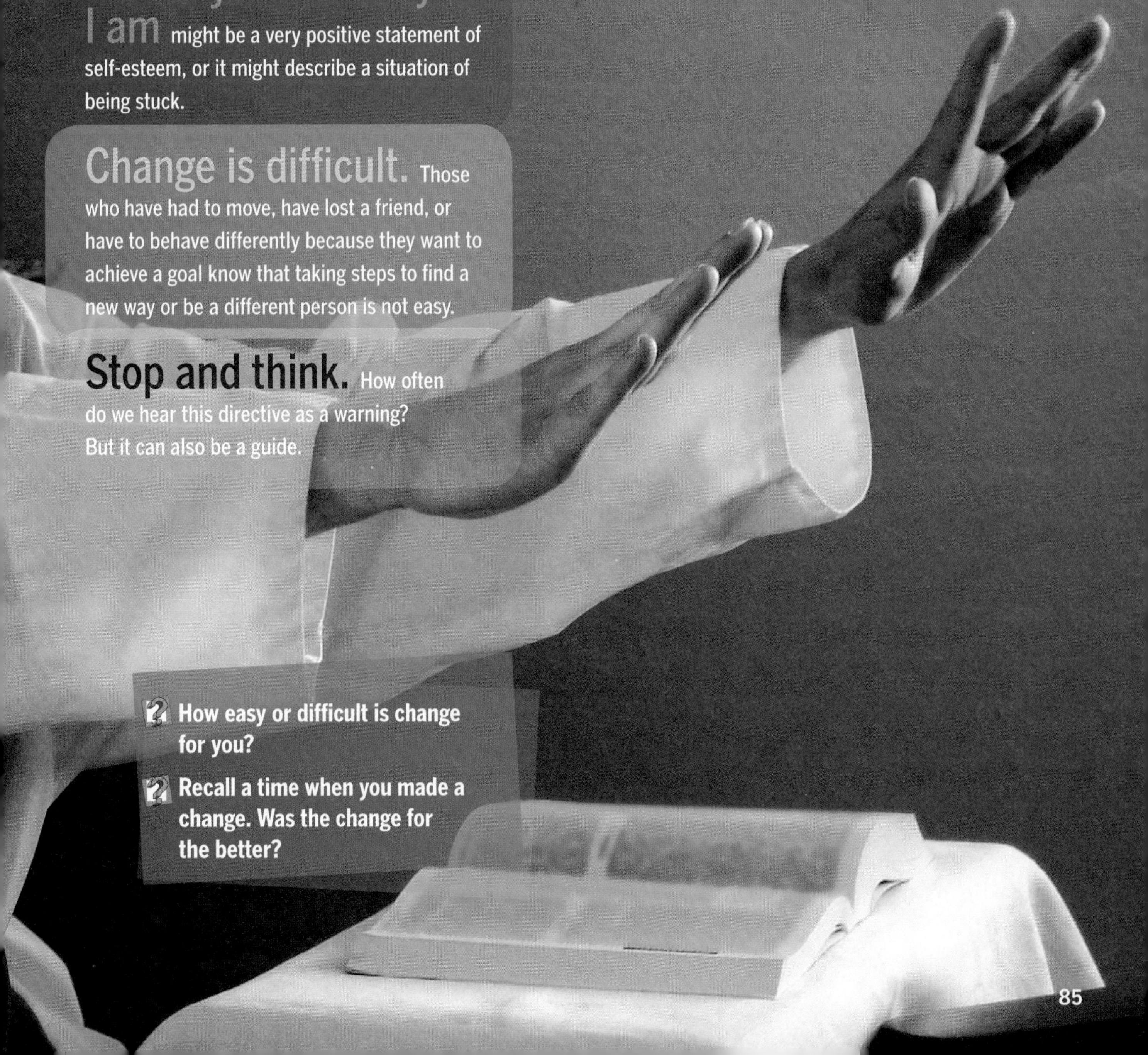

I like myself the way I am might be a very positive statement of self-esteem, or it might describe a situation of being stuck.

Change is difficult. Those who have had to move, have lost a friend, or have to behave differently because they want to achieve a goal know that taking steps to find a new way or be a different person is not easy.

Stop and think. How often do we hear this directive as a warning? But it can also be a guide.

- How easy or difficult is change for you?
- Recall a time when you made a change. Was the change for the better?

Gathering Rite

Procession with the Word

Sing together.

Turn to me, O turn and be saved,
says the Lord, for I am God;
there is no other, none beside me.
I call your name.

"Turn to Me," © 1999, John B. Foley, SJ and GIA Publications.
Published by OCP Publications

Leader: Let us pray.

All: *Pray the Sign of the Cross together.*

Celebration of the Word

Leader: Loving God, we often neglect the gifts of our Baptism and turn from you to sin. We pray to your Holy Spirit to open our hearts and change us that your grace may be renewed in us.

All: Amen.

Leader: A reading from the holy Gospel according to Luke.

All: Glory to you, Lord.

Leader: *Read Luke 22:31–34, 54–62.*
The Gospel of the Lord.

All: Praise to you, Lord Jesus Christ.

Reflect silently.

 How would you feel if you were Peter?

RITUAL FOCUS

Examination of Conscience

Leader: Lord Jesus, you redeemed us by your passion and raised us to new life in Baptism. Send the Holy Spirit to help us reflect on our choices, our actions, and our thoughts as preparation to receive the Sacrament of Penance and Reconciliation.

Use this quiet time to examine your conscience.

Is my heart set on God above everything else?

Am I faithful to the commandments?

Have I been careful to grow in the understanding of my faith?

Do I keep Sundays and feast days holy by participating at Mass?

Do I have a real love for my neighbor, or do I use people for my own ends?

Do I contribute to the well-being and happiness of my family?

Do I share my possessions with the less fortunate? Am I honest and hard-working?

Have I been truthful and fair or have I injured others?

Leader: God gives us an example of love; even when we sin, he loves us. Let us pray.

All: ***Respond after each petition with the prayer,* Lord have mercy.**

Leader: Lord, like Peter we have relied on our strength rather than on grace.

Lord, at times our pride and foolishness have led us into temptation.

Lord, we have been vain and self-important.

Lord, we have been pleased rather than saddened by the misfortunes of others.

Lord, we have shown indifference for those in need.

Lord, we have been afraid to stand up for justice and truth.

Let us pray as Jesus has taught us.

Pray the Lord's Prayer together.

Going Forth

Leader: Lord our God, give us strength to turn from our sins and to serve you in the future with greater love and devotion. Look on us with love and hear our prayer, for you live and reign forever.

All: Amen.

Adapted from Rite of Penance, Appendix II and III

Sing again the opening song.

Examination of Conscience

Reflect on the Celebration

Your Confirmation Reflections

Use these phrases as a starting point for personal reflection.

* *The celebration helped me think about . . .*
* *When I examined my conscience, this is what I learned about myself . . .*

Faith Sharing

With a partner or in a small group, brainstorm additional phrases to add to the list in the examination of conscience on pages 86–87. Discuss the benefits of making an examination of conscience a consistent practice in a young person's life, especially in preparation for receiving the Sacrament of Reconciliation.

SYMBOL OF THE HOLY SPIRIT

Hand When Jesus healed the sick and blessed people, he laid hands on them. (See *Mark 6:5, 8:23, 10:16.*) Later, the Apostles imposed hands on those who were receiving the Holy Spirit. The Letter to the Hebrews lists the imposition of hands among the "fundamental elements" of its teaching. (See *Hebrews 6:2.*) Today, when we celebrate the sacraments, the priest or bishop always extends his hands as a sign of the outpouring of the Holy Spirit.

When are some times you have seen or experienced the laying on of hands in the sacraments?

sin

It may surprise you that we are talking about sin as you prepare to celebrate the Sacrament of Confirmation. We have reviewed the meaning of Baptism and reflected on what it means to be a disciple and a child of God. We have talked about being sealed with the Holy Spirit, receiving the Gifts of the Holy Spirit, and being holy. Even though we have all these gifts, we still turn away from God. We *sin*. We fail to follow the Ten Commandments, and we find it difficult to always follow Jesus' Great Commandment to love God and our neighbor. *Mortal sin* is grave (very serious) by which someone turns completely away from God, breaking his or her relationship with God. *Venial sin* weakens or wounds a person's relationship with God.

As you prepare for Confirmation, there are two reasons to think about sin. One is to be more aware that the Holy Spirit is with you to help you turn away from sin and sinful behavior and attitudes. The other is to spend time taking a look at your life to prepare to celebrate the Sacrament of Reconciliation before you are confirmed.

REFLECT

When do you experience your conscience acting in you? What feelings or thoughts do you associate with your conscience?

conscience

An important work of the Holy Spirit is leading us to conversion. Through the power of the Holy Spirit, individual people and groups (large and small) are given the opportunity and grace to move away from sin and toward God. But conversion and grace require us to cooperate with the Holy Spirit. One of the ways we do this is through an examination of conscience. *Conscience* is our inner capacity to recognize what is right and wrong. It is the internal voice that urges us to do good and avoid evil. An examination of conscience is always a part of the preparation for the Sacrament of Reconciliation. Many people examine their consciences on a daily or weekly basis because they want to strengthen their relationship with God the Father, the Son, and the Holy Spirit.

Forgiveness

SCRIPTURE BACKGROUND

Parables Parables are short stories with a double meaning. The stories are about familiar subjects but also have spiritual meaning. Often they challenge and confront the listener. They might also console the listener. Jesus used parables as teaching tools. The stories he told caused people to turn away from sin and to understand the purpose of a faithful life. His parables described the kingdom of God and conveyed the true nature of God as both demanding and loving and generous in mercy and forgiveness.

FAITH FOCUS

What does Scripture teach us about sin and forgiveness?

The Good News of the Gospel is that God loves us and wants to heal and forgive us. Jesus spent his public life welcoming and eating and drinking with sinners. His presence with Zaccheus and the Samaritan woman caused each of them to repent and change. When he healed people, Jesus often told them their sins were forgiven. This angered some of the Pharisees. They wondered where he got his authority to forgive sins, since only God could do that.

In the parables, Jesus described a forgiving God. He used the image of the shepherd who went out to find the lost sheep, the woman who searched for her lost coin, and the father who waited for his lost son and welcomed him back into the family even after he wasted his inheritance. After Jesus taught the Lord's Prayer, he emphasized that his followers are called to be forgiving people.

Jesus with Disciples in the Temple, 15th Century, Artist Unknown

Called to Forgive

"For if you forgive others their trespasses, your heavenly Father will also forgive you; but if you do not forgive others, neither will your Father forgive your trespasses." . . . Then Peter came and said to him, "Lord, if another member of the church sins against me, how often should I forgive? As many as seven times?" Jesus said to him, "Not seven times, but I tell you, seventy-seven times."

—Matthew 6:14–15, 18:21–22

Jesus' response to Peter's question about how many times we are called to forgive is very challenging. We are called to forgive over and over again.

During the time of Jesus' passion and death, the disciples, except for John, abandoned him. They hid for fear that they too would be persecuted or worse. After the Resurrection, Jesus appeared to them. He not only offered them peace and forgiveness, but he also gave them the power of the Holy Spirit to forgive sins.

DISCUSS

How would you feel if you were in trouble and your friends either abandoned you or denied they knew you? What would it take for you to forgive them?

Jesus Appears to the Disciples

When it was evening on that day, the first day of the week, and the doors of the house where the disciples had met were locked for fear of the Jews, Jesus came and stood among them and said, "Peace be with you." After he said this, he showed them his hands and his side. Then the disciples rejoiced when they saw the Lord. Jesus said to them again, "Peace be with you. As the Father has sent me, so I send you." When he had said this, he breathed on them and said to them, "Receive the Holy Spirit. If you forgive the sins of any, they are forgiven them; if you retain the sin of any, they are retained."

—John 20:19–23

? How is Jesus a model of forgiveness in this Scripture passage?

? What does this Scripture passage say to you about forgiveness?

Share the Word

In small groups, select one of the following Scripture stories and discuss what might have been the outcome of the story if Jesus had never come upon the scene.

- Zacchaeus (Luke 19:2–9)
- Samaritan Woman (John 4:1–42)
- Disciples (John 20:19–23)
- Peter (John 21:15–18)

Discuss situations in daily life in which "showing up" creates opportunities for forgiveness.

Forgiveness and Reconciliation

FAITH FOCUS

What is the role of the Holy Spirit in forgiveness and reconciliation?

REFLECT

What personal or world events would you choose as examples of reconciliation?

With great sincerity, I would like to tell you that forgiveness is the last word spoken by those who truly love. Forgiveness is the highest sign of the capacity to love as God does, for he loves us and therefore constantly forgives us.

John Paul II, in a meeting with Roman youth, March 25, 1999

Jesus empowered his disciples to forgive sins by breathing on them and sending the gift of the Holy Spirit. The Holy Spirit guides and enlightens us. It is through the power of the Holy Spirit that we recognize sin—the habits, attitudes, and actions that are leading us away from living as the children of light we are called to be through Baptism. In the Sacrament of Penance, when we are truly sorry for our sins and want to repair the damage they have caused, our sins are forgiven through the prayers and actions of the priest and the power of the Holy Spirit.

Forgiving others

In the Sacrament of Penance, we ask *forgiveness* for our sins and God grants it. But there are situations in our lives when we are the ones who need to forgive. Maybe a friend betrayed a confidence, or a parent broke a promise, or a sibling "borrowed" something without asking. We might be angry or hurt and find it hard to forgive. Why is that? Because forgiveness means we have to be very generous with our love. We have to forgive as we have been forgiven. The gift of the Holy Spirit at Baptism and Confirmation gives us the strength to forgive. It is that strength that helped Pope John Paul II forgive his would-be assassin. It is that strength that is helping Rwandans, through processes of reconciliation hearings, to live with neighbors who killed their families.

Reconciliation

Reconciliation means to come back together again. It is a process of ending a conflict in such a way that two people or two groups can say: "We forgive and we will start over." Another name for the Sacrament of Penance is the Sacrament of Reconciliation because, through it, we become one again with God, with ourselves, and with others. We confess our sin, we are sorry, we agree to change and perform a penance, we are forgiven, and we are sent forth to share this peace with others.

At the conclusion of the Sacrament of Confirmation, just before the Liturgy of the Eucharist, the deacon or minister prays that we as the Church of God will be a sign and witness of reconciliation:

For the holy Church of God,
in union with [Name] our pope, [Name] our bishop,
and all the bishops,
that God, who gathers us together by the Holy Spirit,
may help us grow in unity of faith and love
until his Son returns in glory:
let us pray to the Lord.
Response: *Lord, hear our prayer.*

For all men,
of every race and nation,
that they may acknowledge the one God as Father,
and in the bond of common brotherhood
seek his kingdom,
which is peace and joy in the Holy Spirit:
let us pray to the Lord.
Response: *Lord, hear our prayer.*

Rite of Confirmation, 30

CATHOLIC SOURCES

Forgiveness Were there no forgiveness of sins in the Church, there would be no hope of life to come or eternal liberation.
Let us thank God who has given his Church such a gift.

Saint Augustine, Sermo 213

SIGNS OF FAITH

Absolution In the Sacrament of Reconciliation, through the absolution of the priest, God forgives or takes away a person's sins and the eternal punishment due because of mortal sins. The power to absolve sin was given to the Apostles and their successors by Jesus. (See *John 20:23*.) Only a validly ordained priest or bishop (the only ministers of this sacrament) can absolve a person who has confessed his or her sin. The person must be sorry and willing to make up for his or her sin in order to be absolved.

Why is it important to you to receive absolution?

Witnesses of Faith

Journeys Past

Saint Francis of Assisi (1181–1226)

Saint Francis of Assisi by Simone Martini

1181 Giovanni Francesco Bernardone is born, the son of a rich cloth merchant of Assisi.

1191–1202 He is a pleasure-seeking, popular leader of the young people in Assisi.

1202 Taken as a prisoner in the war between Assisi and Perugia, he becomes seriously ill.

1205 He experiences a vision from a crucifix in which he is told to "Go, Francis, and repair my house, which as you see is falling into ruin."

1206 Francis makes a pilgrimage to Rome; upon his return, he is denounced by his father as a lunatic and is disinherited. He repairs the Church of San Damiano and dedicates himself to the poor.

1209 He founds the Franciscans.

1212 Francis sets out for Syria and Morocco to convert the Saracens and is shipwrecked. He returns to evangelize Central Italy. Claire of Assisi becomes Francis' spiritual student.

1217 The Franciscans hold their first general meeting with 5,000 in attendance.

1223 They build the first Christmas crèche (nativity scene).

1224 Francis receives the stigmata.

1226 He dies at Assisi.

1228 He is canonized a saint.

"I have been all things unholy. If God can work through me, he can work through anyone."

Your Journey

Life and Dignity of the Human Person

Faith in Action

Jesus' message of compassion for all and loving one's enemies contributed to his arrest and ultimate death. Peter was afraid that might happen to him if he didn't disown Jesus. Francis of Assisi had already gone to war twice—the second time to the Crusades—before he realized that God's way to peace was reconciliation, not war. His father and friends disowned him, but Francis was convinced that Muslims were no less children of God than Christians. Risking his life, he begged both the pope and the sultan to stop the Crusades.

Visit **www.harcourtreligion.com** to discover more about Catholic social teachings.

Journeys Today

Living Witness

When I was growing up, I had a very strong response to the Genesis story as I heard it read and preached in my religion classes and at Church. "God is the Creator of each one of us. God looks at all of us and says we are very good." At the same time, I had two friends, a boy and a girl, one Jewish, the other Protestant. We became a triumvirate. We never thought about our differences. I came to believe that we are all connected based on the oneness of God, in whom all of humanity is inextricably connected.

I do not pray at times. I pray all the time. I pray that the good God will help me be an ambassador of peace and reconciliation wherever I am and whomever I am with.

I started out as a police detective and worked with runaways and gang members. I organized a human relations department in a large city in Missouri and shortly after the city's civil disorder, became its first director. I'm the first African-American to serve as a department head in that city. I have acted as a consultant for peace and reconciliation in a variety of settings. In a way these things "happened to me." I did not seek them out, but I live in prayer that God will help me be an ambassador of peace and reconciliation wherever I am and whomever I am with. And God is so good.

Alvin B.

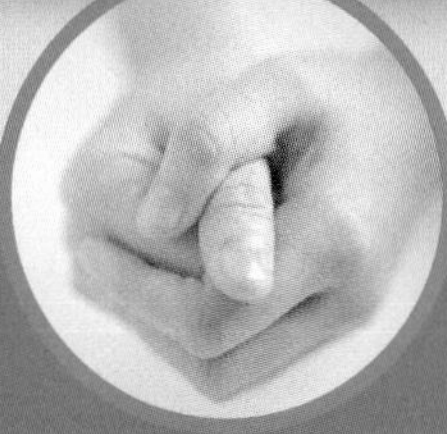

Personal Prayer

Prayer is the lifting of our hearts and minds to God. It is what helps us come to know God and his will for us. It is the lifeline and nurturer of our friendship with God. It is how we communicate with him. As with all communication, prayer involves talking, listening, deep silence, rituals, and gestures. We pray to praise God, to say we are sorry, to ask for things for ourselves and for others, and to express gratitude. God the Holy Spirit teaches us to pray. Though we can pray always about anything, it is also important to set aside time each day to listen for what God is communicating to us.

Faith Walk

Respond in Faith

Your Confirmation Reflections

* Choose a situation in your world (family, friends, work) that is in need of forgiveness and reconciliation. Reflect and write about the place of forgiveness in that situation. What is your responsibility in that situation to forgive or accept forgiveness? What would happen if everyone in that situation worked together to build an environment of peace and joy?
* Conclude your writing with a prayer to the Holy Spirit.

Faith Sharing

In small groups discuss the part of this session that

- most interested you
- most challenged you

Spend some time in group silence thinking about what this session is calling you to change or strengthen in your relationship with God, yourself, or others. At the appropriate time, share this with the group.

closing prayer

Leader: Lord God, we long to be your witnesses throughout the earth.

All: Lord, make me an instrument of your peace!
Where there is hatred, let me sow love.
Where there is injury, pardon.
Where there is discord, harmony.
Where there is doubt, faith.
Where there is despair, hope.
Where there is darkness, light.
Where there is sorrow, joy.

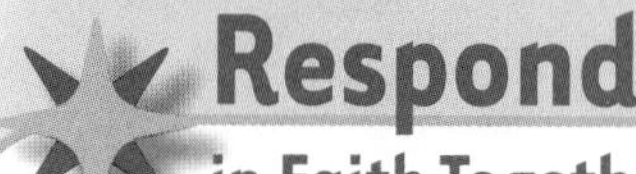

Respond in Faith Together

FAITH FOCUS

Discuss the following beliefs together. Focus on how these beliefs have or could have an effect on your lives today. Refer to the lesson, if necessary.

- Sin is turning away from God. Our sins can be mortal or venial.
- An important work of the Holy Spirit is conversion.
- We are called to forgive and to reconcile.

RITUAL FOCUS

During the celebration, the candidates experienced an examination of conscience. Review the Examination of Conscience on pages 86–87 and together add any appropriate reflection statements.

ACT TOGETHER

Choose one of the following activities to do together:

- View a movie that has forgiveness and reconciliation as a theme and discuss it afterward.
- Find a local organization that has a mission of reconciliation and unity and volunteer to work there for a two- to three-hour period.
- Research groups and organizations that work for international reconciliation. Choose one of them for follow-up.

Your Plan Write about the activity or project you chose:

BEING CATHOLIC

Together: Explore these quotes by famous Catholics and discuss how they relate to sin and forgiveness in your lives.

"There is more joy in heaven over a converted sinner than over a righteous person standing firm."

— Gregory the Great

"The place to start is with ourselves. We will never be credible mediators of forgiveness and peace to others unless we have some very profound sense of peace within ourselves."

— Doris Donnelly

"Reconciliation should be accompanied by justice, otherwise it will not last."

— Corazon Aquino

Faith Walk

Personal prayer Talk about the story in **Journeys Today.**

- ▶ Discuss the notion of praying always and what it means for you.
- ▶ Share the kinds and types of prayer you most practice and enjoy.
- ▶ Visit a local Catholic bookstore and view the various books available on the subject.

Together: Reflect on your experience of forgiveness and reconciliation.

- What helped you forgive?
- What are your obstacles to forgiving?

challenged by the Spirit

How we are with food is how we are with life. Some people eat to survive. Some eat to be nourished, some to be comforted, some to be energized. Some hoard their food. Some share their food.

People use all kinds of food images to describe life situations:

I devoured it.
She lapped it up.
He has an appetite for . . .

Eating and food are universal experiences. Having enough or not having enough are not.

- **What role does eating have for you? For your family?**
- **Recall an experience when sharing a meal with others nurtured your body and spirit.**

Gathering Rite

Procession with the Word

Sing together.

Somos el cuerpo de Cristo.
We are the body of Christ.
Hemos oído el llamado;
we've answered "Yes,"
to the call of the Lord.

"Somos el Cuerpo de Cristo," © 1994, Bob Hurd and Jaime Cortez. Published by OCP Publications

Leader: Let us pray.

All: *Pray the Sign of the Cross together.*

Leader: God our Father, we are your children. Through your Son, Jesus, we are united with you and one another as one family. Through the power of the Holy Spirit, strengthen us to live out our mission as your disciples to bring life to others. We ask this through Jesus Christ our Lord.

All: Amen.

Celebration of the Word

Leader: A reading from the holy Gospel according to John.

All: Glory to you, Lord.

Leader: *Read John 6:35–58.*
The Gospel of the Lord.

All: Praise to you, Lord Jesus Christ.

Reflect silently.

What does the image of the Bread of Life suggest to you about your relationship with Jesus?

RITUAL FOCUS

Sharing a Meal

Be seated around the table.

Leader: Blessed are you almighty Father, who gives us our daily bread.
Blessed is your only begotten Son, who continually feeds us with the word of life.
Blessed is the Holy Spirit, who brings us together at this table of love.
Blessed be God now and forever.

All: Amen.

***Book of Blessings*, 1069**

Share food and conversation at the table.

Going Forth

Bow your heads and pray for God's blessing.

Blessing for Mission

Leader: My brothers and sisters, let us pray that God who is love will enkindle our hearts with the fire of the Holy Spirit, to give us an ardent love for others, like Christ's love for us.

***Book of Blessings*, 586**

All: *Pray silently.*

Leader: Blessed are you, Lord, God of mercy, who through your Son gave us a marvelous example of charity and the great commandment of love for one another. Send down your blessings on these your servants, who so generously devote themselves to helping others. When they are called on in times of need, let them faithfully serve you in their neighbor. We ask this through Christ our Lord.

All: Amen.

***Book of Blessings*, 587**

Sing again the opening song.

Blessing for Mission

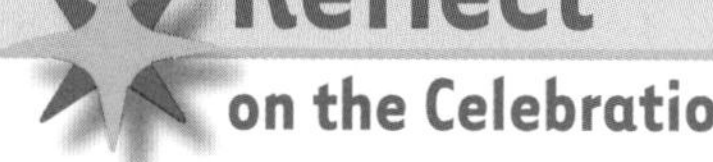

Reflect on the Celebration

Your Confirmation Reflections

* Describe your experience of sharing a meal in the context of prayer.
* Would this celebration have been different if you had participated in it during the first session of the Confirmation process?
* What are the similarities and differences between this celebration and the celebration of the Eucharist?

Faith Sharing

Reflect silently on the words of the blessings in the celebration. Choose the word or phrase that is most important to you. With a partner or in a small group, share the phrase and the reason you chose it. Discuss the blessings you will need to serve the needs of others.

SYMBOL OF THE HOLY SPIRIT

Finger of God The hymn *"Veni, Creator Spiritus"* is one of the oldest and most widely used hymns in the Church. In it the Holy Spirit is referred to as the finger of God in the verse "Thou, finger of God's hand we own." There are references to the finger of God in both the Old and New Testaments. The Ten Commandments are said to be written by the "finger of God" *(Exodus 31:18)*. In the New Testament, Jesus talks about casting out devils by the finger of God's hand. (See *Luke 11:20*.) The *Catechism of the Catholic Church* also makes reference to the Scripture verse ". . . you are a letter of Christ, . . . written not with ink but with the Spirit of the living God, not on tablets of stone but on tablets of human hearts" *(2 Corinthians 3:3)* as a reference to this title of the Holy Spirit.

How does the image of being a letter about Christ written by the Holy Spirit make you feel? What do you think people who might "read" you as a letter would learn about Christ?

Journey of Initiation

We began this preparation for Confirmation using the image of a faith journey. We make this journey with fellow travelers. Through the Sacraments of Initiation, we become members of the Church, which is both the *Body of Christ* and a *pilgrim people*. In Baptism we were joined to one another in the Body of Christ.

> *From all who are baptized in water and the Holy Spirit, you have formed one people, united in your Son, Jesus Christ.*
>
> **Rite of Baptism, 118**

Through Baptism we also became sharers in the priesthood of Christ and in his prophetic and royal *mission*. We have a purpose. We are being sent to be an example to others and to witness to Jesus Christ in words and actions in family, work, and the larger community.

Confirmation completes our baptismal grace. Through it, our bond with the Body of Christ, the Church, is strengthened and deepened. We are given special strength of the Holy Spirit to help us in our mission of witness. Confirmation brings with it an obligation to spread and explain the faith to others.

DISCUSS

How is the experience of sharing special meals with family members or friends different from eating alone, or grabbing a snack?

Meals on the Journey

Meals are an important part of a journey. People who set out on a long trip together often plan how, what, and when they are going to eat. Mealtime for them is a special time. They regroup as travelers, and they are fed and strengthened by food and companionship. The Sacrament of Eucharist is the sacred meal for the pilgrim people. Every Sunday we come together as a worshiping community at the table of the Lord to be nourished by the Body and Blood of Jesus Christ under the appearances of bread and wine. While Baptism and Confirmation are received only once in a person's life, we come to the Lord's table over and over again. Each time we participate in the Eucharist, we are nourished and strengthened as individuals and a community. We continue the work of our public witness to the mission of the Body of Christ in the world.

Meals of Jesus

SCRIPTURE BACKGROUND

Cup of Blessing The Passover meal, which Jesus celebrated with his Apostles, was divided into four parts. Each part was marked by the blessing over a cup of wine. The first was a festival blessing *(kiddush)* spoken over the first cup of wine, followed by the serving of a dish of herbs. The second included a recital of the Passover narrative and the "Little Hallel" (*Psalm 113*), followed by the drinking of the second cup of wine. The third course was the main meal, consisting of lamb and unleavened bread, after which Jesus and the Apostles drank the third cup of wine, known as the "cup of blessing." The Passover climaxed with the singing of the "Great Hallel" (*Psalms 114–118*) and the drinking of the fourth cup of wine.

Some New Testament scholars identify the cup blessed and distributed by Jesus at the Last Supper as the third cup in the Passover meal because of the Scripture passage that immediately follows: "When they had sung a hymn . . ." (*Mark 14:26*). Paul identifies this "cup of blessing" with the Eucharistic cup (*1 Corinthians 10:16*).

FAITH FOCUS

What does Scripture teach us about the Eucharist?

Our knowledge of and belief in Jesus' real presence in the Eucharist and the celebration of the Eucharist as a meal and a sacrifice are rooted in the Scriptures. In the Gospel of John, when the people ask for a sign, Jesus refers to himself as the Bread of Life. The Gospel portrays Jesus giving a very clear description of what he means by that image. It is difficult for some of his followers to believe what he is telling them and they turn away. (See *John 6:35–58.*) Even when this happens, Jesus remains firm in his teaching.

The Gospels describe many situations in which Jesus is at a meal. He provides meals for people. He preaches and teaches at them. He eats with sinners and outcasts. He even uses the image of a meal to describe what the kingdom is like. During his public life, he and his friends and followers dined together often. On the night before he died, Jesus ate the Last Supper with his Apostles. It is this meal that the Scriptures identify as Jesus' own Body and Blood; his sacrifice on the cross is the meal of the new covenant.

Last Supper

Then he took a loaf of bread and when he had given thanks, he broke it and gave it to them, saying, "This is my body, which is given for you. Do this in remembrance of me." And he did the same with the cup after supper, saying, "This cup that is poured out for you is the new covenant in my blood . . ."

—Luke 22:19–20

The Walk to Emmaus

After the crucifixion and Resurrection, Jesus appeared to his followers around meal settings. The Apostles who were returning to Emmaus had a long discussion with him about the events of his death and Resurrection, but they did not recognize him until he was at the table.

He took bread, blessed and broke it, and gave it to them. Then their eyes were opened, and they recognized him; and he vanished from their sight. They said to each other, "Were not our hearts burning within us while he was talking to us on the road, while he was opening the scriptures to us?" That same hour they got up and returned to Jerusalem; and they found the eleven and their companions gathered together. They were saying, "The Lord has risen indeed, and he has appeared to Simon!" Then they told what had happened on the road, and how he had been made known to them in the breaking of the bread.

—Luke 24:30–35

The meal at Emmaus Accademia, Vence, Italy by Marco Marziale (1489–1507)

Early Church

Early Church members identified themselves as the Body of Christ and used the phrase "breaking of the bread" as a name for the Eucharist.

Day by day, as they spent much time together in the temple, they broke bread at home and ate their food with glad and generous hearts, praising God and having the goodwill of all the people.

—Acts 2:46–47

Saint Paul

Saint Paul wrote his first letter to the church at Corinth to challenge and remind them that being the Body of Christ was a call to unity and sacrifice.

The cup of blessing that we bless, is it not a sharing in the blood of Christ? The bread that we break, is it not a sharing in the body of Christ? Because there is one bread, we who are many are one body, for we all partake of the one bread.

—1 Corinthians 10:16–17

What do these Scripture readings tell you about the Eucharist?

Which of these Scripture readings best describes your understanding of the Eucharist?

Share the Word

In small groups, read the following Gospel stories about the feeding of the multitudes and compare them by creating a list of similarities and differences.

- Matthew 14:13–21
- Mark 6:30
- Luke 9:10–17
- Matthew 15:32–39
- Mark 8:1–10
- John 6:1–14

Confirmation and Eucharist

FAITH FOCUS

What is the connection between Confirmation, Eucharist, and mission?

The Holy Spirit
came down upon the disciples
and set their hearts on fire with love:
may he bless you,
keep you one in faith and love
and bring you to the joy of God's kingdom.
Amen.

Rite of Confirmation, 49

DISCUSS

What images or experiences does the phrase "communion with God" raise for you?

When you celebrate Confirmation, you will have celebrated all the Sacraments of Initiation. You will be a full member of the Church. But Confirmation is not the end. Initiation into the Paschal Mystery of Jesus and the life of the Church never ends. It plunges us into a lifelong relationship of communion with God and his people. Though the rituals of initiation are limited in time and space, they lead us into a much richer and deeper reality of union with the Father, Son, and Holy Spirit. The Eucharist is an ongoing Sacrament of Initiation. There is no graduation. As fully initiated Catholics, we are called to live for Christ as disciples and heirs to God's kingdom. We are promised the gift of eternal life. We come to the Lord's table each week to be fed and nurtured. We become what we eat—the Body of Christ.

Mystagogy

Even though we use words and phrases such as "full" members of and "fully initiated" into the Body of Christ, we do not always recognize what those words and phrases mean, nor do we always live by them. We are talking about a mystery. It is a mystery that we are one with Christ, that we possess the Gifts of the Holy Spirit, and that God is present in our lives and the life of the world. We cannot explain these things, but we believe. The Greek word *mystagogy* means "to uncover the mysteries." We are not capable of fully grasping the mystery of initiation. When we spend time in prayer and reflection, thinking about what happens to us as we celebrate the Sacraments of Initiation and experiencing the presence of the Living God in our lives, we engage in mystagogy. We gradually see the greatness of the calling to live as the Body of Christ.

Mission

In Baptism all Christians are called to *mission*. A mission is a task. The task of baptized Christians is to continue the work of Christ in the world according to God's plan. It is our mission to help people come to know the love that exists in the Father, Son, and Holy Spirit and to better appreciate God's love for them. The Holy Spirit guides and energizes us for this mission. When we are faithful to this mission, we will find true happiness. People come to know God's love and salvation through the actions of the Church—through our actions. In the document *Renewing the Vision: A Framework for Catholic Youth Ministry*, the Bishops of the United States have identified eight components of Catholic youth ministry. As you think about your mission, use these components and reflect on your gifts and ways you can further the mission of the Church.

REFLECTION FOR MISSION

		I Can
Advocacy	Speaking on behalf of various groups, such as families, the poor, the elderly	
Catechesis	Participating in activities to learn more about Scripture and the Doctrines of the Church	
Community Life	Participating in the parish community and building an environment of love, support, and an appreciation of diversity	
Justice and Service	Working for justice, serving those in need, pursuing peace, and defending the rights and dignity of others	
Evangelization	Inviting people into a deeper relationship with Jesus, the Risen Lord, and helping them live as his disciples	
Leadership	Calling forth and affirming the gifts and talents of others	
Pastoral Care	Being a compassionate presence and outreach to others who are hurting and in need	
Prayer and Worship	Praying and worshiping with others to deepen everyone's relationship with Jesus Christ through communal and liturgical prayer	

CATHOLIC SOURCES

Evangelii Nuntiandi One of the most important contemporary encyclicals about the mission of evangelization states: "It is often said nowadays that the present century thirsts for authenticity. Especially in regard to young people it is said that they have a horror of the artificial or false and that they are searching above all for truth and honesty. These 'signs of the times' should find us vigilant. Either tacitly or aloud—but always forcefully—we are being asked: Do you really believe what you are proclaiming? Do you live what you believe? Do you really preach what you live? The witness of life has become more than ever an essential condition for real effectiveness in preaching. Precisely because of this we are, to a certain extent, responsible for the progress of the Gospel that we proclaim." (76)

SIGNS OF FAITH

Bread and Wine Bread and wine are staple foods for humans. They are almost universally accepted as signs of nourishment and celebration. At Mass we use unleavened bread that is made without yeast and wine that is made from grapes. At the altar, by the power of the Holy Spirit and the prayers and actions of the priest, the bread and wine become the Body and Blood of Jesus. They become our spiritual food.

When you approach the altar to be nourished by the Body and Blood of Jesus, what do you want to be nourished for?

Witnesses of Faith

Journeys Past

Blessed Mother Teresa
(1910–1997)

1910 Agnes Gonxha Bojaxhiu is born in Skopje, Macedonia.

1922 At the age of twelve, she feels the call to be a missionary.

1928 She goes to Dublin, Ireland, and joins the Sisters of Loreto, an Irish community with missions in India.

1931–1948 Teresa takes her first vows and teaches at St. Mary's High School in Calcutta. There the suffering and poverty she observes make such a deep impression on her that she asks to leave the convent school and devotes herself to working among the poor.

1948 She becomes an Indian citizen and without any funds she begins an open-air school for slum children. She is joined by volunteers and receives financial support, which makes it possible to extend her work.

1950 Mother Teresa founds the Missionaries of Charity to work with the poor. Their primary task is to love and care for those persons who had no one to care for them.

1971 She receives the Pope John XXIII Peace Prize.

1972 She receives India's Jawaharlal Nehru Award for International Understanding.

1996 She receives honorary U.S. citizenship.

1997 Mother Teresa dies.

2003 Pope John Paul II beatifies Mother Teresa.

"Do not wait for leaders; do it alone, person to person."

Your Journey

Option for the Poor and Vulnerable

Faith in Action

Blessed Mother Teresa lived as a saintly example of Micah 6:8—she acted with justice, loved tenderly, and walked humbly with God. Like Jesus, she focused her love especially on those who were poor and vulnerable. We can, too, especially when we get to know at least one of these special children of God and make them an important part of our lives. Besides sharing some of our time and perhaps our resources with such persons, we can take our new awareness of their needs and become their advocates. Whether it's local agencies, the state legislature, and/or the U.S. Congress that need to act, we can add our voices on their behalf.

Visit **www.harcourtreligion.com** to discover more about Catholic social teachings.

Journeys Today

Living Witness

In my junior year of high school I was involved in a service project where we served meals to the homeless. I did it because I had to, and it was difficult for me. I did not like being around the homeless; I was afraid of them.

During that time I participated in a retreat where one of the facilitators said something that startled me. "Christ is in the homeless and Christ is in the poor." I thought about my response to the homeless people. I began to pray that my fear would go away and that my attitude would change. I began to actually talk to people and listen to their stories and when the hours for my service time were completed, I continued volunteering at the homeless shelter until I went off to college and law school.

Before I took the bar exam, I attended the "Red Mass," which is a special Mass to pray for God's blessing on judges, lawyers, and others who protect and administer the law. The sermon at that Mass focused on the law and the Christian's response to the poor. I decided to make another retreat after I took the bar exam but first I had to get through that. In between the grueling days of that exam, I met a man sitting next to me at a café who advised, "There is always another test." That's not what I wanted to hear—but he was right. The retreat led me to a decision to be a lawyer for and with the poor.

Andrew G.

Retreat

Faith Walk

In general, a retreat is a reflective time away from the ordinary activities of daily life. A religious retreat is a time of prayer and meditation. Some retreats are done in solitude and silence; others in a group with a great deal of conversation. A retreat might be done in a parish or a remote location either privately or at a retreat center such as a monastery or house of prayer. While many people go away to a retreat house or participate in a scheduled and structured retreat at the parish, such as the retreat you may be involved in as part of your Confirmation preparation, you can also make your own retreat. Schedule some time for yourself to "be on retreat" in a quiet place at home or in another quiet comfortable place, where you will not be distracted. Take your Bible and your own personal notebook and spend some time reflecting on one of the Psalms or one of the stories of Jesus.

Respond in Faith

Your Confirmation Reflections

As you prepare to live as a full member of the Body of Christ, write your personal mission statement. Use these three questions as a guide:

*Who am I?

*What do I want to do?

*How will I do it?

Faith Sharing

In small groups discuss the part of this session that

- ▶ most interested you
- ▶ most challenged you

Spend some time in group silence thinking about what this session is calling you to change or strengthen in your relationship with God, yourself, or others. At the appropriate time, share this with the group.

closing prayer

Lord God, send us forth as your Body, strengthened by the power and presence of your Holy Spirit. Teach us your ways and guide us to do your will for the sake of the world and all of our brothers and sisters. May we live in such a way that others will come to know you and your healing and generous presence. We ask this in your name. Amen.

Respond in Faith Together

FAITH FOCUS

Discuss the following beliefs together. Focus on how these beliefs have or could have an effect on your lives today. Refer to the lesson, if necessary.

- The Church is the Body of Christ and a pilgrim people.
- Through Confirmation our bond with the Church is strengthened and we receive the special strength of the Holy Spirit to help us be witnesses.
- The Eucharist nourishes and strengthens us for mission.

RITUAL FOCUS

During the celebration, the candidates experienced the sharing of a meal and blessing for mission. Share a special meal together and thank each other for the support and sharing during this period of preparation.

ACT TOGETHER

Choose one of the following activities to do together:

- Plan and prepare a meal for family members and/or friends. As part of the meal, develop a simple ritual of breaking bread and sharing a recent experience of Christ's presence.
- Volunteer to work at a soup kitchen or serve meals at a Catholic Worker House.
- Research world hunger. Choose a project in this field that you can continue to be involved in together after Confirmation.

Your Plan Write about the activity or service project you chose:

BEING CATHOLIC

Together: Discuss these quotes from famous Catholics. Focus on how they apply to your life.

"If we but paused for a moment to consider attentively what takes place in this Sacrament, I am sure that the thought of Christ's love for us would transform the coldness of our hearts into a fire of love and gratitude."

— Saint Angela of Foligno

"By our little acts of charity practiced in the shade we convert souls far away, we help missionaries, we win for them abundant alms; and by that means build actual dwellings spiritual and material for our Eucharistic Lord."

— Saint Therese of Lisieux

"Happy is the soul that knows how to find Jesus in the Eucharist, and the Eucharist in all things!"

— Saint Peter Julian Eymard

Faith Walk

Retreats Talk about the story in **Journeys Today.**

- Identify areas in your life where you feel called to act for others.
- Share any retreat experiences you may have.
- Discuss why retreats are helpful to nourish faith life.

Together: Reflect on your experiences of being strengthened and nurtured to live the Christian life. Discuss what actions can be taken to strengthen your spiritual health.

Faith Discernment

Answer the following questions by circling the response—Y (yes), N (no), or U (undecided)—that most indicates your belief or practice.

I see my life as a spiritual journey.	Y	N	U
I can name ways that God is present in my life.	Y	N	U
I like being Catholic.	Y	N	U
I have felt God's forgiveness.	Y	N	U
I have felt God's healing presence.	Y	N	U
I have invited non-Catholic friends to come to church with me.	Y	N	U
I pray every day.	Y	N	U
I practice some form of meditation.	Y	N	U
I have read one spiritual book in the last year.	Y	N	U
I celebrate the Sacrament of Reconciliation (Confession, Penance) more than once a year.	Y	N	U
I attend Mass every Sunday or Saturday and on Holy Days of Obligation.	Y	N	U
I support my parish financially.	Y	N	U
Within the last year, I have participated in at least one church activity other than the Sacraments or Religious Education.	Y	N	U
I give of my time and talent to help others.	Y	N	U
I own a Bible.	Y	N	U
Sometimes I use Scripture to help me pray.	Y	N	U
Sometimes reading Scripture helps me change my life.	Y	N	U
Sometimes I hear God's voice in the Scripture readings and homilies at Mass.	Y	N	U
There are three divine Persons in one God: the Father, Son, and Holy Spirit.	Y	N	U
Jesus was fully human and fully divine.	Y	N	U
Jesus rose from the dead.	Y	N	U
God the Holy Spirit descended upon the Apostles at Pentecost.	Y	N	U
God the Holy Spirit is alive in me.	Y	N	U
The Immaculate Conception is about Mary's birth.	Y	N	U
Mary is the Mother of God.	Y	N	U

Saints are models and witnesses of how to live a Christian life.	Y	N	U
There are seven Sacraments.	Y	N	U
There are ten Commandments.	Y	N	U
There are six Holy Days of Obligation.	Y	N	U
There are five Precepts of the Church.	Y	N	U
There are eight Beatitudes.	Y	N	U
Jesus Christ is truly and really present in the consecrated bread and wine.	Y	N	U
The Sacraments of Initiation are Baptism, Confirmation, and Eucharist.	Y	N	U
The Pope is the Vicar of Christ on earth.	Y	N	U
Mortal sin cuts us off from a relationship with God and the Church.	Y	N	U
The Sacrament of Baptism takes away original sin.	Y	N	U
Marriage is a sacrament between a man and a woman.	Y	N	U
Artificial birth control is against the teaching of the Church.	Y	N	U
Catholics believe in the sacredness of all life, which includes among others: unborn babies, the sick and elderly, and prisoners on death row.	Y	N	U
I believe racism is a sin.	Y	N	U
I am concerned about the problems of the poor.	Y	N	U
I actively work for peace.	Y	N	U
I contribute to caring for the environment.	Y	N	U
Christian values are important to me when I consider the morality of nuclear weapons and war.	Y	N	U
I practice the Spiritual and Corporal Works of Mercy.	Y	N	U
I know what a moral decision is.	Y	N	U
I pray to the Holy Spirit when I make a moral decision.	Y	N	U
I consider the Church's teachings when I make a moral decision.	Y	N	U
I find the Church's teachings on sexual morality helpful in my own life.	Y	N	U
I talk with others when I am making a serious moral decision.	Y	N	U

Your Sponsor/Mentor

Tips for Developing Your Relationship

During the preparation time:

- Write out a job description for your sponsor/mentor.
- Determine with your sponsor/mentor when you will meet for faith sharing after each session. Make sure you set aside specific times to talk. That doesn't mean you always have to hold a formal meeting. Sometimes the best discussions may take place at informal and spontaneous times. If appropriate make a "date" to do something you will both enjoy doing together. You will find suggested activities in the Journey Together section of the *Candidate Book.*
- Show your sponsor/mentor the job description you have written for him or her and discuss both of your expectations for your roles.
- Find out if your sponsor/mentor is involved in some kind of service in the parish or community and, if appropriate, volunteer to go with him or her to see what happens.
- Periodically attend Mass with your sponsor/mentor and talk about the readings and homily afterward.
- When you meet individually with your sponsor/mentor, determine together the best way for you to pray, such as using a formal prayer, a spontaneous prayer, reflection on a Scripture reading, or one of the prayers or blessings in the *Sponsor & Mentor Handbook* or *Candidate Book.*
- During your time together, you and your sponsor/mentor will share your faith together. Don't be puzzled or perplexed by the term *faith sharing.* You probably do a lot of it in everyday conversation. Faith sharing encompasses talking about the beliefs, values, and meanings that shape your life because you are a believer and a practicing Roman Catholic.
- Do not hesitate to share any questions, concerns, or doubts you may have with your sponsor/mentor. He or she is there to listen to, support, and guide you.
- Think of yourself and your sponsor/mentor as companions on a faith journey. The image of companioning is key to creating the environment of faith sharing. Companions actively listen to and trust each other. They are going in the same direction. They assist each other with experience, skill, and sharing. They enjoy each other and the journey.
- Ask for your sponsor/mentor's opinions. Few things compliment us more than being asked our opinion.

After the celebration:

When the formal process of Confirmation is over, you and your sponsor/mentor may want to continue as faith companions. Here are some suggestions on how to do this:

- Share your experience of the celebration with your sponsor/mentor.
- Use e-mail or phone conversations to continue faith sharing and building your relationship.
- Continue or begin a new service project together. It does not have to be long term. Perhaps a one-time event would be better.
- Remember and celebrate the anniversary of your Confirmation.

spiritual health inventory

Reflect on your experiences of being strengthened and nurtured to live the Christian life. Look over the inventory below and check where you are today. Discuss with your sponsor/mentor, your parents, or a friend what actions you can take to strengthen your spiritual health.

	A Strength	Doing Fine	Needs Work	A Weakness
Makes time for personal prayer				
Participates in Sunday Eucharist				
Receives the Sacrament of Reconciliation frequently				
Nurtures a spirit of gratitude and generosity				
Admits faults and wrongdoing				
Accepts forgiveness and forgives others				
Seeks opportunities for conversion				
Respects the sanctity of life				
Respects and protects the rights of others				
Cultivates a love for justice and peace				
Studies and prays with Scripture				
Appreciates the doctrines of the Church				
Fosters an awareness of God's presence in creation				
Acts on moral values				
Serves others willingly				

Discerning Vocation

As you journey through your Confirmation sessions, you will read the stories of eight people who have found a "calling" or a *vocation*. The word *vocation* comes from the Latin *vocare*, which means "to call."

Vocation

The idea of a vocation is central to the Christian belief that God creates each of us with gifts and talents oriented toward specific purposes and a way of life. In the Catholic Church, this idea of vocation is especially associated with a divine call to service to the Church and humanity through particular vocational life commitments such as marriage to a particular person, consecration as a religious, ordination to priestly ministry in the Church, or a holy life as a single person. In the broader sense, Christian vocation includes the use of one's gifts in work, family life, church, or civic commitments for the sake of the Gospel or in response to questions such as: "What is God's will for me?" "What is my mission?" "How can I best live out my baptismal calling?"

You are at an age when people begin to seriously think about what their vocation might be. In their book *Sustaining the Spirit*, Catherine Cronin Carotta and Michael Carotta talk about three vocational calls: call of work, call of relationships, and call of faith. They say: *Responding to any of these vocational callings is transformative and reflects a spiritual pursuit. The vocational journey is a spiritual one because it is all about your life, but still not about a life that is yours. . . . It is a spiritual journey that enables us to make meaning of the ordinary and sense the sacredness of it.* (p. 14)

Journeys Today

Read the stories in the Journeys Today sections of your *Candidate Book* and think about the following questions:

- Which call or calls do they reflect?
- How did the spiritual practice described in the Faith Walk help each person discern his or her vocation?
- Which of the stories do you most identify with?

Reflection Exercise

Reflect on the following questions. You may want to write your responses in your own personal notebook.

- Do I have a long-standing desire to be or to do something for or with others?
- What am I passionate about?
- Am I drawn to the priesthood or religious life?
- Do I want to be married and to be a parent?
- Do I feel drawn to a career of service?

Gifts and Talents Inventory

Look over the list of gifts and talents below. Circle those that you see evident in yourself. Ask yourself how the ones you chose might affirm what you are thinking about as your vocational choice. Discuss them with your sponsor/mentor or a friend and ask for their feedback.

Artistic	Good with numbers	
Athletic	Helpful	Reflective
Brave	Honest	Religious
Bright	Intelligent	Responsible
Caring	Just	Steadfast
Creative	Kind	Spiritual
Decisive	Listener	Talkative
Dependable	Likes children	Trustworthy
Desires to help the poor	Observant	Unique
Easygoing	Open-minded	Willing to make sacrifices
Energetic	Prayerful	____________________
Generous	Peacemaker	____________________

Tips for Discerning Your Vocation

- Pray to the Holy Spirit for guidance
- Talk it over with your parents and friends.
- If you feel drawn to the priesthood or religious life, call the diocesan vocation director or the vocation director of the religious community you are interested in and talk with them.
- Talk to people you would like to be like and ask them about their own vocational journeys. Don't be afraid to ask. They will probably be complimented by your interest.
- Do volunteer work in the areas you are considering—babysitting, being a school aid, working as an apprentice, going on a mission trip, working with the poor—and reflect on how that experience is for you.
- Find a spiritual director or spiritual companion.
- Go on a retreat.

Interview Reflection

At some time during your preparation, you will be interviewed by your catechist, parish priest, or Confirmation coordinator. Here are some questions for you to reflect on as you prepare for your interview. You may wish to use the blank spaces to jot down any significant points, issues, or concerns you want to bring up during the interview. The best way to make this interview valuable for you and the person who interviews you is to speak honestly about your thoughts and feelings.

1. What does receiving the Sacrament of Confirmation mean for you in your life today? (Include your expectations, your concerns, and your hopes.)

2. Was your experience of working with a sponsor helpful or not? (Include specific examples.)

3. What did you learn about the Catholic faith that you did not know before? (Include facts, insights, and feelings.)

4. Which parts of the sessions did you find most helpful for your own faith development and understanding? What made it helpful?

5. How do you experience the presence and power of the Holy Spirit?

6. Which of the Gifts of the Holy Spirit do you most want to have deepened or strengthened in your life? Why?

7. How has your practice of prayer grown during your preparation time? What are you intending to do to continue your prayer life after you are confirmed?

8. What effect did being of service to others have on you during this period of time? How will you continue that aspect of your Christian life?

9. What actions will you take to be a more active member of your parish after you are confirmed?

10. What questions or concerns would you like to discuss with the person who interviews you?

order of the rite of confirmation

The essential rite of Confirmation is the anointing with sacred chrism on the forehead. This gesture is accompanied by the laying on of hands and the words: "Be sealed with the Gift of the Holy Spirit." (9)

In order to keep the fundamental connection of Confirmation to Baptism and the Eucharist as Sacraments of Initiation, there is a renewal of baptismal promises during the celebration of Confirmation and it is preferred that Confirmation be celebrated within the Mass so all can participate in the Eucharist since "Christian initiation reaches its culmination in the communion of the body and blood of Christ." (13)

Liturgy of the Word

The Liturgy of the Word is celebrated in the ordinary way. The readings for the Liturgy of the Word may be chosen from the Mass of the day, the Lectionary (nos. 763–767), or from the Rite itself (nos. 61–75).

Sacrament of Confirmation

Presentation of the Candidates

After the reading of the Gospel, the pastor, another priest, deacon, or catechist presents the candidates for Confirmation; usually each candidate is called by name and comes forward with his or her sponsor or parent or stands for the presentation.

Homily or Instruction

The bishop gives a brief homily to help the whole assembly understand the meaning of Confirmation.

Renewal of Baptismal Promises

After the homily, the candidates stand and renew their baptismal promises before the bishop or priest.

Bishop: *Do you reject Satan and all his works and all his empty promises?*

Candidates: *I do.*

Bishop: *Do you believe in God the Father almighty, creator of heaven and earth?*

Candidates: *I do.*

Bishop: *Do you believe in Jesus Christ, his only Son, our Lord,*
who was born of the Virgin Mary,
was crucified, died, and was buried,
rose from the dead,
and is now seated at the right hand of the Father?

Candidates: *I do.*

Bishop: *Do you believe in the Holy Spirit,*
the Lord, the giver of life,
who came upon the apostles at Pentecost
and today is given to you sacramentally in confirmation?

Candidates: *I do.*

Bishop: *This is our faith. This is the faith of the Church.*
We are proud to profess it in Christ Jesus our Lord.

Rite of Confirmation, 23

The Laying on of Hands

The bishop and the concelebrating priests stand together and lay hands on all the candidates by extending their hands over them. The bishop alone prays the prayer asking God for the Gifts of the Holy Spirit.

My dear friends:
in baptism God our Father gave the new birth of eternal life
to his chosen sons and daughters.
Let us pray to our Father
that he will pour out the Holy Spirit
to strengthen his sons and daughters with his gifts
and anoint them to be more like Christ the Son of God.

All pray in silence for a short time.

Rite of Confirmation, 24

The bishop and priests extend their hands while the bishop alone sings or says:

All-powerful God, Father of our Lord Jesus Christ,
by water and the Holy Spirit
you freed your sons and daughters from sin
and gave them new life.
Send your Holy Spirit upon them
to be their Helper and Guide.
Give them the spirit of wisdom and understanding,
the spirit of right judgment and courage,
the spirit of knowledge and reverence.
Fill them with the spirit of wonder and awe in your presence.
We ask this through Christ our Lord.

All: *Amen.*

Rite of Confirmation, 25

The Anointing with Chrism

Each candidate goes before the bishop. The sponsor places his or her right hand on the candidate's shoulder and gives the candidate's name to the bishop, or the candidate may give his or her own name.

The bishop dips his right thumb in the chrism, makes the Sign of the Cross on the candidate's forehead, and says:

Bishop: *[Name], be sealed with the Gift of the Holy Spirit.*

Candidate: *Amen.*

Bishop: *Peace be with you.*

Candidate: *And also with you.*

Rite of Confirmation, 27

General Intercessions

Intercessions are offered for those who were confirmed, their parents and godparents, the Church, and the world.

Liturgy of the Eucharist

At the conclusion of the General Intercessions, the Liturgy of the Eucharist continues according to the Order of Mass except the profession of faith is omitted, since it has already been made, and some of the newly confirmed may bring the gifts to the altar.

Blessing

Instead of the usual blessing, the bishop prays a special blessing over the people:

God our Father
made you his children by water and the Holy Spirit:
may he bless you
and watch over you with his fatherly love.

All: *Amen.*

Jesus Christ the Son of God
promised that the Spirit of truth
would be with his Church for ever:
may he bless you and give you courage
in professing the true faith.

All: *Amen.*

The Holy Spirit
came down upon the disciples
and set their hearts on fire with love:
may he bless you
keep you one in faith and love
and bring you to the joy of God's kingdom.

All: *Amen.*

May almighty God bless you,
the Father, and the Son, and the Holy Spirit.

All: *Amen.*

Rite of Confirmation, 33

Prayer Over the People

Instead of the preceding blessing, the bishop may pray the following prayer over the people:

God our Father,
complete the work you have begun
and keep the gifts of the Holy Spirit
active in the hearts of your people.
Make them ready to live his Gospel
and eager to do his will.
May they never be ashamed
to proclaim to all the world Christ crucified
living and reigning for ever and ever.

All: *Amen.*

Rite of Confirmation, 33

celebrating reconciliation

Rite for Reconciliation of Individual Penitents

Preparation of Priest and Penitent

Before celebrating the Sacrament of Reconciliation, both the priest and penitent prepare themselves by prayer to celebrate the sacrament. ". . . penitents should compare their own life with the example and commandments of Christ and then pray to God for the forgiveness of their sins." (15)

Penitents may choose to meet with the priest face-to-face or behind a screen.

Welcoming the Penitent

The priest welcomes the penitent and the penitent makes the Sign of the Cross.

Reading of the Word of God

The priest or the penitent may read a text of holy Scripture, or this may be done as part of the preparation for the celebration of the sacrament.

Penitent's Confession and Acceptance of the Penance

The penitent confesses his or her sins to the priest. The priest may encourage the penitent to be sincerely sorry and give practical advice. Then the priest gives a penance that is meant to atone for past sin and be "an aid to a new life and an antidote for weakness." (18)

Penitent's Prayer and the Priest's Absolution

The penitent expresses sorrow for sin and a resolve to begin a new life using a traditional Act of Contrition or other words.

Then the priest extends his hands over the penitent's head and says:

God, the Father of mercies,
through the death and resurrection of his Son
has reconciled the world to himself
and sent the Holy Spirit among us
for the forgiveness of sins;
through the ministry of the Church
may God give you pardon and peace,
and I absolve you from your sins
in the name of the Father, and of the Son, and of the Holy Spirit.

Penitent: *Amen.*

Rite of Penance, 46

Proclamation of Praise and Dismissal of the Penitent

After the absolution, the priest prays:

Give thanks to the Lord, for he is good.

Penitent: *His mercy endures for ever.*

Rite of Penance, 47

choosing a name

In some dioceses, those to be confirmed are given the option to choose a separate Confirmation name. Although a centuries-old, popular practice for those baptized as infants but confirmed later, choosing another name for Confirmation is not mentioned in the Confirmation Rite or the *Code of Canon Law*. There is no obligation to select a Confirmation name that is different from the name given at Baptism.

Importance of Names

Your parents probably spent many hours thinking about what they would name you. Your name may have been chosen to honor a relative or a saint who is revered by your family or culture. While it is customary to use the names of saints as baptismal names, the Church now permits other names as long as they are not incompatible with Christian faith. However your baptismal name was chosen, it is now a part of your history and identity.

Names are important in our religious tradition as well. In the Old Testament, God promises David: ". . . and I will make for you a name, like the name of the great ones of the earth" (*1 Chronicles 17:8*). The prophet Isaiah, speaking in God's name, proclaims to King Cyrus, "it is I, the Lord . . . I call you by your name" (*Isaiah 45:3–4*). In the New Testament, Jesus tells the disciples that their names are written in heaven (see *Luke 10:20*) and both the Letter to the Philippians (*4:3*) and the Book of Revelation (*21:12–14*) refer to names being written in the book of life.

A Confirmation Name

Taking a new name at Confirmation can be symbolic of a new or deeper stage in your faith life. There are several Scripture stories of people whose names changed after they experienced a conversion: Abram to Abraham, Jacob to Israel, Simon to Peter, and Saul to Paul. Celebrating the Sacrament of Confirmation is an opportunity for you to reflect on what Baptism and union with Christ through the power of the Holy Spirit in Confirmation means in your life. It is also an occasion to reflect on how you want to witness to the power of the Holy Spirit in your life. If you choose a name other than your baptismal name, look to saints and holy people who are truly witnesses of faith for you. Choose the name of a saint you admire and whom you want to be your patron. The decision to choose a special patron (and name) at Confirmation or to honor the name received at Baptism is not really the most important part of the celebration. What is important is God and the Church's commitment to you through the gift of the Holy Spirit.

choosing a sponsor

The Role of the Sponsor

The most important role of a Confirmation sponsor is to walk with you and guide you as you prepare to receive the fullness of the Holy Spirit in this Sacrament of Initiation.

Confirmation sponsors are like spiritual coaches or mentors. They affirm your strengths and point out ways you can grow and become better in the practice of faith. You share your faith journey together. A Confirmation sponsor participates in your preparation and presents you to the bishop or the priest during the celebration of the Sacrament of Confirmation.

Depending on your parish program, your sponsor may:

- attend some of the catechetical sessions
- participate in retreats or service projects with you
- spend time with you doing the activities on the *Journey Together* pages, which guide you both in sharing how the teachings and practices of the Church relate to your lives

How to Choose a Sponsor

Choosing a sponsor for Confirmation is an important task. You may choose one of your godparents or you may choose another person. When you think about choosing a Confirmation sponsor, think about choosing someone who is an active, practicing Catholic; someone who is enthusiastic about the Catholic faith; and someone who is easy to talk to and be around.

Here are some suggestions to help you as you make your choice:

- Think about the qualities you want your sponsor to have.
- Think about people who are good examples for you.
- Ask yourself if one of your godparents would be a good sponsor.
- Talk with your parents, other family members, or your catechist about who would be a good choice.
- Remember, sponsors must be at least sixteen years old. They must be practicing Catholics and have already celebrated Baptism, Confirmation, and Eucharist.
- Pray to the Holy Spirit.
- Talk with the person you select and explain why you chose him or her and what his or her responsibilities will be.

Catholic Prayers and Practices

As Catholics we have many prayers and practices to help us grow as disciples of Jesus. Some of these prayers and practices are central or core, such as the celebration of sacraments, the recitation of the Creed, and our belief in the communion of saints. Throughout the history of the Church, believers have gathered as an assembly to celebrate these core beliefs in the **liturgical or public prayer** of the Church when they celebrated the sacraments and prayed the Liturgy of the Hours. They also developed other prayers and practices called **devotions**, which help us express the mystery of the rich faith contained in those central or core prayers and practices.

The Sacrament of the Eucharist

The **Mass** is the most important liturgical prayer of the Catholic Church. In the Eucharist, the Church expresses praise and thanks to God for all the gifts he has given us, especially the gift of his Son, Jesus. For many years, throughout the world, the Mass was celebrated only in Latin. The Second Vatican Council ushered in the option to celebrate Mass in the vernacular or the language of the people. Some parishes provide the opportunity to celebrate the whole Mass in Latin, and many parishes sing some of the important prayers of the Mass in Latin.

Mass Prayers

Sign of the Cross In the name of the Father, and of the Son, and of the Holy Spirit. Amen.	**Signum Crucis** In nómine Patris, et Fílii, et Spíritus Sancti. Amen. (Latin)
I confess to almighty God, and to you, my brothers and sisters, that I have sinned through my own fault, in my thoughts and in my words, in what I have done, and what I have failed to do; and I ask blessed Mary, ever virgin, all the angels and saints, and you, my brothers and sisters, to pray for me to the Lord our God. Amen.	**Confiteor** Deo omnipotenti, beatae Mariae semper Virgini, beato Michaeli Archangelo, beato Ioanni Baptistae, sanctis Apostolis Petro et Paulo, et omnibus Sanctis, quia peccavi nimis cogitatione, verbo et opere: mea culpa, mea culpa, mea maxima culpa. Ideo precor beatam Mariam semper Virginem, beatum Michaelem Archangelum, beatum Ioannem Baptistam, sanctos Apostolos Petrum et Paulum, et omnes Sanctos, orare pro me ad Dominum Deum nostrum. Amen. (Latin)
Lord, have mercy. **Lord, have mercy.** Christ, have mercy. **Christ, have mercy.** Lord, have mercy. **Lord, have mercy.**	Kyrie eleison. **Kyrie eleison.** Christe eleison. **Christe eleison.** Kyrie eleison. **Kyrie eleison. (Greek)**
Glory to God in the highest, and peace to his people on earth. Lord God, heavenly King, almighty God and Father, we worship you, we give you thanks, we praise you for your glory. Lord Jesus Christ, only Son of the Father, Lord God, Lamb of God, you take away the sins of the world: have mercy on us; you are seated at the right hand of the Father: receive our prayer. For you alone are the Holy One, you alone are the Lord, you alone are the Most High, Jesus Christ, with the Holy Spirit, in the glory of God the Father. Amen.	**Gloria** in excelsis Deo et in terra pax hominibus bonae voluntatis. Laudamus te, benedicimus te, adoramus te, glorificamus te, gratias agimus tibi propter magnam gloriam tuam, Domine Deus, Rex caelestis, Deus Pater omnipotens Domine Fili unigenite, Iesu Christe, Domine Deus, Agnus Dei, Filius Patris, qui tollis peccata mundi, miserere nobis; qui tollis peccata mundi, suscipe deprecationem nostram. Qui sedes ad dexteram Patris, miserere nobis. Quoniam tu solus Sanctus, tu solus Dominus, tu solus Altissimus, Iesu Christe, cum Sancto Spiritu in gloria Dei Patris. Amen. (Latin)

We believe in one God, the Father, the Almighty, maker of heaven and earth, of all that is seen and unseen. We believe in one Lord, Jesus Christ, the only Son of God, eternally begotten of the Father, God from God, Light from Light, true God from true God, begotten, not made, one in Being with the Father. Through him all things were made. For us men and for our salvation he came down from heaven: by the power of the Holy Spirit he was born of the Virgin Mary, and became man. For our sake he was crucified under Pontius Pilate; he suffered, died, and was buried. On the third day he rose again in fulfillment of the Scriptures; he ascended into heaven and is seated at the right hand of the Father. He will come again in glory to judge the living and the dead, and his kingdom will have no end. We believe in the Holy Spirit, the Lord, the giver of life, who proceeds from the Father and the Son. With the Father and the Son he is worshiped and glorified. He has spoken through the Prophets. We believe in one holy, catholic and apostolic Church. We acknowledge one baptism for the forgiveness of sins. We look for the resurrection of the dead, and the life of the world to come. Amen.	**Credo** in unum Deum, Patrem omnipotentem, factorem caeli et terrae, visibilium omnium et invisibilium. Et in unum Dominum Iesum Christum, Filium Dei unigenitum, et ex Patre natum ante omnia saecula. Deum de Deo, Lumen de Lumine, Deum verum de Deo vero, genitum non factum, consubstantialem Patri; per quem omnia facta sunt. Qui propter nos homines et propter nostram salutem descendit de caelis. Et incarnatus est de Spiritu Sancto ex Maria Virgine, et homo factus est. Crucifixus etiam pro nobis sub Pontio Pilato, passus et sepultus est, et resurrexit tertia die, secundum Scripturas, et ascendit in caelum, sedet ad dexteram Patris. Et iterum venturus est cum gloria, iudicare vivos et mortuos, cuius regni non erit finis. Et in Spiritum Sanctum, Dominum et vivificantem, qui ex Patre Filioque procedit.Qui cum Patre et Filio simul adoratur et conglorificatur: qui locutus est per prophetas. Et unam, sanctam, catholicam et apostolicam Ecclesiam. Confiteor unum baptisma in remissionem peccatorum. Et expecto resurrectionem mortuorum, et vitam venturi saeculi. Amen. (Latin)
Holy, holy, holy Lord, God of power and might, heaven and earth are full of your glory. Hosanna in the highest. Blessed is he who comes in the name of the Lord. Hosanna in the highest.	**Sanctus, Sanctus, Sanctus,** Dominus Deus Sabaoth. Pleni sunt caeli et terra gloria tua. Hosanna in excelsis. Benedictus qui venit in nomine Domini. Hosanna in excelsis. (Latin)
Our Father, who art in heaven, hallowed be thy name; thy kingdom come; thy will be done on earth as it is in heaven. Give us this day our daily bread; and forgive us our trespasses as we forgive those who trespass against us, and lead us not into temptation, but deliver us from evil. Amen.	**Pater Noster** qui es in cælis: sanctificétur Nomen Tuum; advéniat Regnum Tuum; fiat volúntas Tua, sicut in cælo et in terra. Panem nostrum cotidianum da nobis hódie; et dimítte nobis débita nostra, sicut et nos dimíttimus debitóribus nostris; et ne nos indúcas in tentatiónem; sed líbera nos a Malo. Amen. (Latin)
Lamb of God, you take away the sins of the world: have mercy on us. Lamb of God, you take away the sins of the world: have mercy on us. Lamb of God, you take away the sins of the world: grant us peace.	**Agnus Dei,** qui tollis peccata mundi, miserere nobis. Agnus Dei, qui tollis peccata mundi, miserere nobis. Agnus Dei, qui tollis peccata mundi, dona nobis pacem. (Latin)

Blessed Sacrament

During Mass, through the power of the Holy Spirit and the prayers and actions of the priest, the bread and wine become the Body and Blood of Jesus. This is called **real presence**. Many prayers and devotions developed from the faithful's devotion to the real presence of Jesus in the Eucharist:

Prayer before the Blessed Sacrament

This is a popular traditional Catholic devotion that honors the Catholic belief in real presence. We reserve the Blessed Sacrament in the tabernacle for the sick, the dying, and for people who want to stop in and pray.

Throughout the history of the Church, believers developed other prayers and practices that helped them express the mystery of the rich faith contained in those central or core prayers and practices.

A Prayer Before the Blessed Sacrament

Lord, give to our hearts the light of faith and the fire of love, that we may worship in spirit and in truth our God and Lord, present in this sacrament.

We ask this through Christ our Lord.

Amen.

Rite of Eucharistic Exposition and Benediction, 227

Communion of the Sick

The Church provides frequent opportunities for those who are sick and homebound to receive the Eucharist. The priest, deacon, or extraordinary minister of Holy Communion take Holy Communion that has been consecrated at parish liturgy to the sick in their homes or other places they may be being cared for. Extraordinary ministers of Holy Communion are lay persons appointed when no deacon or priest is available to take Holy Communion.

Benediction

This liturgical action is a devotion to the presence of Jesus Christ in the Eucharist. It is a prayer of adoration. During Benediction, the Blessed Sacrament—contained in a monstrance or ciborium—is exposed and incensed. Prayers and hymns of adoration are said and sung. There is a reading from Scripture and a homily or exhortation is given to help participants understand the mystery of the Eucharist. At the conclusion of the period of adoration, the priest, deacon, or extraordinary minister raises the Blessed Sacrament in a blessing of the participants.

Forty Hours

This devotion to the Blessed Sacrament is a special forty-hour period of continuous prayer made before the Blessed Sacrament in solemn exposition. The focus is upon the presence of Jesus Christ in the Holy Eucharist. It begins with a Solemn Mass of Exposition, which concludes with the exposition of the Blessed Sacrament and a procession. The Blessed Sacrament remains on the altar in a monstrance during the next forty hours while the faithful gather for personal or public prayer in adoration of our Lord.

The Blessed Virgin Mary

As the Mother of Jesus, the Son of God, Mary is called the Mother of God, the Queen of all Saints, and the Mother of the Church. There are many prayers and practices of devotion to Mary.

Magnificat

Also called the Canticle of Mary (see *Luke 1:46–55*), the Magnificat is the Virgin Mary's joyous prayer in response to her cousin Elizabeth's greeting. (See *Luke 1:41–45*.) This great hymn forms part of the Church's prayer in the Liturgy of the Hours. When it is recited as part of the Liturgy of the Hours, it is followed by the Glory to the Father.

My soul proclaims the greatness of the Lord, my spirit rejoices in God my Savior, for he has looked with favor on his lowly servant. From this day all generations will call me blessed: the Almighty has done great things for me, and holy is his Name. He has mercy on those who fear him in every generation. He has shown the strength of his arm, he has scattered the proud in their conceit. He has cast down the mighty from their thrones, and has lifted up the lowly. He has filled the hungry with good things, and the rich he has sent away empty. He has come to the help of his servant Israel for he has remembered his promise of mercy, the promise he made to our fathers, to Abraham and his children forever. **Glory** to the Father and to the Son and to the Holy Spirit, as it was in the beginning, is now, will be forever. Amen	**Magníficat ánima mea Dóminum,** et exsultávit spíritus meus in Deo salvatóre meo, quia respéxit humilitátem ancíllæ suæ. Ecce enim ex hoc beátam me dicent omnes generatiónes, quia fecit mihi magna, qui potens est,et sanctum nomen eius, et misericórdia eius in progenies et progénies timéntibus eum. Fecit poténtiam in bráchio suo, dispérsit supérbos mente cordis sui; depósuit poténtes de sede et exaltávit húmiles. Esuriéntes implévit boniset dívites dimísit inánes. Suscépit Ísrael púerum suum, recordátus misericórdiæ, sicut locútus est ad patres nostros, Ábraham et sémini eius in sæcula. **Glória** Patri et Fílio et Spirítui Sancto. Sicut erat in princípio, et nunc et semper, et in sæcula sæculórum. Amen. (Latin)

The Rosary

One of the most popular devotions to Mary is the Rosary. It is both a meditation and a vocal prayer that focuses on the mysteries or events in the lives of Jesus and Mary. There are twenty mysteries of the Rosary.

Mysteries of the Rosary

The Joyful Mysteries: The Annunciation, The Visitation, The Nativity, The Presentation in the Temple, The Finding in the Temple; **The Luminous Mysteries:** The Baptism of Jesus, The Wedding at Cana, The Proclamation of the Kingdom, The Transfiguration, The Institution of the Eucharist; **The Sorrowful Mysteries:** The Agony in the Garden, The Scourging at the Pillar, The Crowning with Thorns, The Carrying of the Cross, The Crucifixion and Death; **The Glorious Mysteries:** The Resurrection, The Ascension, The Descent of the Holy Ghost, The Assumption, The Coronation in Heaven.

Prayers of the Rosary

There are five basic prayers to know when praying the Rosary:

Apostles' Creed
I believe in God, the Father, almighty, creator of heaven and earth.
I believe in Jesus Christ. He was conceived by the power of the Holy Spirit and born of the Virgin Mary. He suffered under Pontius Pilate, was crucified, died and was buried. He descended to the dead. On the third day, he rose again. He ascended into heaven, and is seated at the right hand of the Father. He will come again to judge the living and the dead.
I believe in the Holy Spirit, the holy catholic Church, the communion of saints, the forgiveness of sins, the resurrection of the body, and life everlasting. Amen.

Our Father, who art in heaven, hallowed be thy name; thy kingdom come; thy will be done on earth as it is in heaven. Give us this day our daily bread; and forgive us our trespasses as we forgive those who trespass against us, and lead us not into temptation, but deliver us from evil. Amen.

Hail Mary
Hail Mary, full of grace,
the Lord is with thee.
Blessed art thou among women,
and blessed is the fruit of thy womb, Jesus.
Holy Mary, Mother of God,
pray for us sinners, now and at the hour of our death.
Amen.

Glory to the Father and to the Son and to the Holy Spirit, as it was in the beginning is now, and ever shall be world without end. Amen.

Hail, Holy Queen, Mother of Mercy, our life, our sweetness and our hope. To you do we cry, poor banished children of Eve; to thee do we send up our sighs, mourning and weeping in this valley of tears. Turn then, most gracious advocate, thine eyes of mercy toward us, and after this our exile, show unto us the blessed fruit of thy womb, Jesus.
O clement, O loving, O sweet Virgin Mary!

Pray for us, O holy Mother of God. That we may be worthy of the promises of Christ.

How to Pray the Rosary

1. Pray the Sign of the Cross and say the Apostles' Creed.
2. Pray the Our Father.
3. Pray three Hail Marys.
4. Pray the Glory to the Father.
5. Say the first mystery; then pray the Our Father.
6. Pray ten Hail Marys while meditating on the mystery.
7. Pray the Glory to the Father.
8. Say the second mystery; then pray the Our Father. Repeat 6 and 7 and continue with the third, fourth, and fifth mysteries in the same manner.
9. Pray the Hail Holy Queen.

Other Ways to Pray

Prayer is the lifting of our hearts and minds to God. There are different kinds of prayer. We may pray prayers of praise, prayers of thanksgiving, prayers of petition, and prayers of intercession. Through prayer we experience union with God. There are also many different ways to pray. We pray with words, with gesture, with song, and in silence. Other prayer styles such as meditation, scriptural prayer, contemplation, and devotional prayer can be done alone or in a group.

Lectio Divina

This is a slow, contemplative praying of the Scriptures, which enables you to spend time with God through reading and meditating on his word in the Scriptures. It involves reading a passage of Scripture, listening quietly to what it is saying, meditating on what you have read and heard, praying or having a conversation with God about what we hear and how that applies to our life, and finally, contemplating or just being in the presence of God. This form of prayer has no other goal than spending time with God through the medium of his word. The amount of time we spend in any of the four steps of *lectio divina*, whether it is reading, meditation, praying, or contemplation depends on God's Spirit.

Novenas

Novenas are nine successive days of either public or private prayer. A novena may be prayed for a special intention, an occasion, or in preparation for a feast. Many novenas are prayers to specific saints or the Blessed Mother. The person or group praying the novena prays a certain prayer or prayers for nine days.

Additional Catholic Prayers

These prayers are prayers that Catholics learn and pray often during their daily lives:

Prayer to the Holy Spirit Come Holy Spirit, fill the hearts of your faithful. And kindle in them the fire of your love. Send forth your Spirit and they shall be created And you will renew the face of the earth.	**Memorare** Remember, O most gracious Virgin Mary, that never was it known that anyone who fled to your protection, implored thy help or sought thy intercession was left unaided. Inspired with this confidence, I fly unto thee, O Virgin of virgins, my Mother. To thee do I come, before thee I stand, sinful and sorrowful. O Mother of the Word Incarnate, despise not my petitions, but in thy mercy hear and answer me. Amen.
Grace Before Meals Bless us O Lord and these your gifts which we are about to receive from your goodness, through Christ our Lord. Amen.	**Act of Faith** O my God, I firmly believe that you are one God in three divine Persons, Father, Son, and Holy Spirit. I believe that your divine Son became man and died for our sins and that he will come to judge the living and the dead. I believe these and all the truths which the Holy Catholic Church teaches because you have revealed them who are eternal truth and wisdom, who can neither deceive nor be deceived. In this faith I intend to live and die. Amen.
Grace After Meals We give you thanks for all your gifts, almighty God, living and reigning now and for ever. Amen.	**Act of Hope** O Lord God, I hope by your grace for the pardon of all my sins and after life here to gain eternal happiness because you have promised it who are infinitely powerful, faithful, kind, and merciful. In this hope I intend to live and die. Amen.
Prayer of Saint Ignatius Take O Lord, all my liberty. Receive my memory, my understanding and my whole will. All that I am, all that I have, you have given me, and I give it back to you, to be used according to your will. Give me only your love and your grace; with these I am rich enough, and I desire nothing more. Amen.	**Act of Love** O Lord God, I love you above all thins and I love my neighbor for your sake because you are the highest, infinite and perfect good, worthy of all my love. In this love I intend to live and die. Amen.

Living as Witnesses

Based on Scriptures and the laws of the Church, Catholics follow these guides and rules to live as disciples and faithful followers of Jesus:

The Ten Commandments

1. I am the Lord your God. You shall not have strange gods before me.
2. You shall not take the name of the Lord your God in vain.
3. Remember to keep holy the Lord's day.
4. Honor your father and your mother.
5. You shall not kill.
6. You shall not commit adultery.
7. You shall not steal.
8. You shall not bear false witness against your neighbor.
9. You shall not covet your neighbor's wife.
10. You shall not covet your neighbor's goods.

Works of Mercy

The Works of Mercy are ways to respond to Jesus when we see him in those who are in need. The Corporal Works of Mercy meet people's physical needs, and the Spiritual Works of Mercy bring spiritual hope and healing.

Corporal

Feed the hungry.
Give drink to the thirsty.
Clothe the naked.
Shelter the homeless.
Visit the sick.
Visit the imprisoned.
Bury the dead.

Spiritual

Counsel the doubtful.
Instruct the ignorant.
Admonish the sinners.
Comfort the afflicted.
Forgive offenses.
Bear wrongs patiently.
Pray for the living and the dead.

Precepts of the Church

The following precepts are important duties of all Catholics.

1. Take part in the Mass on Sundays and holy days. Keep these days holy and avoid unnecessary work.
2. Celebrate the Sacrament of Reconciliation at least once a year if there is serious sin.
3. Receive Holy Communion at least once a year during Easter time.
4. Fast and abstain on days of penance.
5. Give your time, gifts, and money to support the Church.

Holy Days of Obligation

Catholics are required to attend Mass on Sunday unless a serious reason prevents them from doing so. Catholics also must go to Mass on certain holy days. In the United States, the holy days of obligation are the feasts of:

- **Mary the Mother of God (January 1)**
- **the Ascension of the Lord (forty days after Easter or the Sunday nearest the end of the forty-day period)**
- **the Assumption of Mary (August 15)**
- **All Saints' Day (November 1)**
- **the Immaculate Conception of Mary (December 8)**
- **Christmas (December 25)**

Gifts and Fruits

The Gifts of the Holy Spirit are given in Baptism and Confirmation. The Gifts give us power to choose and act as living witnesses. The fruits are the result of the Holy Spirit's action in our lives.

Gifts of the Holy Spirit

Wisdom
Understanding
Right judgment (*Counsel*)
Courage (*Fortitude*)
Knowledge
Reverence (*Piety*)
Wonder and awe (*Fear of the Lord*)

Fruits of the Holy Spirit

Charity
Joy
Peace
Patience
Kindness
Goodness
Generosity
Gentleness
Faithfulness
Modesty
Self-control
Chastity

Virtues

Theological Virtues

The theological virtues are gifts from God. They are called the theological virtues because they are rooted in God, directed toward him, and reflect his presence in our lives.

- **Faith means believing in God and all that he has revealed to us and believing in all that the Church proposes for our belief.**
- **Hope is the desire, bolstered by trust, to do God's will, and achieve eternal life and the graces that make this desire come true.**
- **Through charity, we love God above all else, and our neighbors as ourselves.**

Cardinal Virtues

The cardinal virtues are the principal moral virtues around which all the other virtues and the moral life hinge. In Latin the word *cardo* means hinge. Cardinal virtues help us lead a moral life by governing our actions, controlling our passions and emotions, and keeping our conduct on the right track. These virtues are Prudence, Justice, Fortitude, and Temperance.

Glossary

absolution The forgiveness of sin and the punishment due to sin given by an ordained priest in the Sacrament of Reconciliation.

Advocate A title given to the Holy Spirit that means helper.

Baptism One of the Sacraments of Initiation. It takes away original sin; makes us adopted children of God, members of the Body of Christ, and temples of the Holy Spirit.

Body of Christ A name given to the Church that expresses that Christ is its head and the baptized are the members of the Body.

canonization A lengthy and solemn process through which the Church recognizes someone of heroic virtue a saint.

chrism A combination of olive oil and balsam. It signifies abundance of grace and committed service to God. It is used at Baptism, Confirmation, and Holy Orders.

Christian Sometimes we say the baptized person is *christened*. He or she is then a Christian.

communal The faith of the Church is a shared or communal faith. It is through the community of the Church that our faith is fed and supported.

Confirmation One of the Sacraments of Initiation. It completes the grace of Baptism by a special outpouring of the Gifts of the Holy Spirit, which seal the candidates and enable them to be active participants in the worship and apostolic life of the Church.

conscience The God-given ability that helps individuals know the difference between right and wrong.

conversion A sincere change of mind, heart, and desire to turn away from sin and evil and turn toward God.

convocation A large assembly of people. In reference to the Church, it means a large assembly of people who are called by God's word.

courage The power to stand up for my beliefs and the values of Jesus' message even when it is difficult.

covenant A solemn and sacred agreement between humans or between God and humans.

disciple A student and a believer.

Eucharist The Sacrament of Initiation during which the wine and bread become the Body and Blood of Christ and all who receive him in Holy Communion are brought closer to him and one another.

evangelize To share the Good News of Jesus with others in a way that invites them to believe in him.

Examination of Conscience A process of looking at one's life with the assistance of the Holy Spirit to determine the nature of one's actions, habits, and attitudes toward God and the Church.

faith Believing in God and all that God has revealed. It is a gift, a free response, and a virtue.

forgiveness The gift of the Holy Spirit at Baptism and Confirmation gives us the strength to forgive others. Through the Sacrament of Penance, we ask forgiveness for our sins and God grants it.

Gifts of the Holy Spirit Seven powers and inclinations received in the sacraments of Baptism and Confirmation. They are: wisdom, understanding, right judgment, courage, knowledge, reverence, wonder and awe.

grace The free and undeserved gift God gives us so we can become his adopted children.

holiness A quality possessed when one participates in God's life. God is the source of all holiness.

Holy Spirit The Holy Spirit helps us become stronger children of God and members of the Church.

Incarnation The mystery that the Son of God took on human nature and became man while remaining God in order to save all people.

initiation Means becoming a member.

knowledge The power to know the value and worth of things and see all of life and creation through God's eyes.

marks of the Church The essential characteristics that distinguish the Church and its mission. There are four: one, holy, catholic, and apostolic.

miracle A sign or wonder such as healing, which can take place only through the power of God.

mission A task one is sent to do. The task of baptized Christians is to continue the work of Christ in the world according to God's plan.

missionaries People who answer the call to bring Christ's message to others.

mortal sin A grave (very serious) sin by which someone turns completely away from God. The conditions of mortal sin are: the matter must be serious, the person must know the sinful action is serious, and the person must freely choose to do it.

mystagogy Means to uncover the mysteries. It is also the final period in the Rite of Christian Initiation.

original sin The sin of the first humans, which disrupted the original harmony, goodness, and balance of creation. It wounded and placed humankind in disordered relationships with God, one another, and creation.

Paraclete An English translation of the Greek word, *parakletos*, used in the Scriptures to describe the Holy Spirit; advocate (or intercessor), teacher, helper, comforter, and consoler.

Paschal Candle Also called the Easter candle. It is a reminder that Christ is the Light of the World.

Penance The sacrament in which, through the power of the Holy Spirit and the prayers and actions of the priest, sins are forgiven. It is also called Reconciliation and Confession.

pilgrim people Through the Sacraments of Initiation, we become members of the Church, which is both the Body of Christ and a pilgrim people.

real presence The unique presence of Christ in the Eucharist.

reconciliation Means coming back together. Penance and the Sacrament of Anointing of the Sick are both sacraments of reconciliation because through God's mercy and forgiveness, the sinner is reconciled with God and also the Church.

revelation The self-communication of God especially in his own Son, Jesus Christ.

reverence The power to treat God and people with honor, seeing people as made in God's image.

right judgment The power to make good decisions in matters of right and wrong, good and evil.

sacramentals Sacred symbols and objects that help Catholics respond to the grace received in the sacraments; sacramentals help us to pray and remember God's love for us.

sacraments Instituted by Christ and given to the Church. They are seven visible signs of God's grace.

Sacraments of Initiation The three sacraments that make us full members of the Church: Baptism, Confirmation, and Eucharist.

saint A person who led a holy life giving God glory and who now enjoys eternal life with God in heaven.

Sanctifier Means to *make holy.* It is a title of the Holy Spirit.

sanctifying grace God's divine life within us that makes us his friends and adopted children.

sin An offense against God and the Church.

Trinity The name the Church gives to the mystery of one God in three Persons: Father, Son, and Holy Spirit.

understanding The power to better understand the mysteries of life and religion, to know how to live your life as a follower of Jesus, and to apply the teachings of the Church.

venial sin A less serious sin that weakens, but does not destroy, a person's relationship with God and other people.

wisdom The power to judge things in light of God's standards and to make decisions and act according to God's law.

witness Someone who gives evidence.

wonder and awe The power to recognize how awesome God is and to recognize this awe in his creation.

understanding The power to better understand the mysteries of life and religion, to know how to live our lives as followers of Jesus, and to apply the teachings of the Church.

index

Boldfaced numbers refer to pages on which the terms are defined.